GIDE and HEMINGWAY

Kennikat Press
National University Publications
Literary Criticism Series

General Editor
John E. Becker
Fairleigh Dickinson University

GIDE and HEMINGWAY

Rebels Against God

BEN STOLTZFUS

National University Publications
KENNIKAT PRESS // 1978
Port Washington, N. Y. // London

Manufactured in the United States of America

Published by
Kennikat Press Corp.
Port Washington, N.Y./London

Library of Congress Cataloging in Publication Data

Stoltzfus, Ben Frank, 1927–
    Gide and Hemingway.

    (Literary criticism series) (National university
publications)
    Bibliography: p.
    Includes index.
    1. Gide, André Paul Guillaume, 1869–1951–Criticism
and interpretation. 2. Hemingway, Ernest, 1899–1961–
Criticism and interpretation. I. Title.
PQ2613.I2Z728   809'.04   78-5164
ISBN 0-8046-9214-9

For Jan, Celia, and Andrew;
Mark, Matthew, Sarah, and Stephen

CONTENTS

ACKNOWLEDGMENTS

I am grateful to my colleagues and students whose intelligence, judgment, and wise counsel have added much to my own evaluation of Gide and Hemingway. Special thanks go to Professors Cándido Ayllón, Willis Barnstone, George Knox, and Keith Macfarlane.

Quotations from the works of André Gide are fully protected by French and international copyright, and are used by permission of the Librairie Gallimard. All references to Gallimard editions are from the following: the three-volume Pléiade edition of *Journal 1889-1939* (Paris, 1948), *Journal 1939-1949* (Paris, 1954), *Romans, récits et soties* (Paris, 1958), the one-volume edition of *Théâtre* (1942), the one-volume edition of *Les Cahiers et les poésies d'André Walter* (Paris, 1952), *Oeuvres Complètes*, vol. 4 (Paris, 1932-39), and Albert Camus's *L'Homme révolté* (Paris, 1951).

Permission to quote from Gide in English translation has been authorized by American and British publishers who retain exclusive rights: Random House, Inc. and Secker and Warburg Limited for *The Journals of André Gide, 1889-1949;* Random House, Inc. for *Fruits of the Earth* and Camus's *The Rebel;* Citadel Press and Philosophical Library, Inc. for Gide's *The White Notebook.* Permission to quote from Jean-Paul Sartre's *Situations* (New York: Fawcett, 1965) is authorized by George Braziller, Inc.

Quotations from the works of Ernest Hemingway are fully protected by United States and international copyright, and are used by permission of Charles Scribner's Sons. Permission to quote from Carlos Baker and Hemingway has been granted for the following: Carlos Baker, *Ernest Hemingway: A Life Story* (1969); Hemingway, *Death in the Afternoon* (1932), *Green Hills of Africa* (1935), and *The Old Man and the Sea* (1952). Permission to quote from "On the Blue Water," *Esquire,* 1936, is by permission of Alfred Rice, Esq., executor for Mr. Hemingway's estate.

Permission to reprint the section entitled "Gide the (Im)moralist," which appeared in modified form in *Contemporary Literature,* has been granted by the University of Wisconsin Press. The section entitled "Saul" was first published in modified form in the *French Review* and in *Gide's Eagles.* I wish to thank the editors of the *French Review* and of Southern Illinois University Press for permission to use it. The writing of this book was made possible, in part, by grants from the University of California Humanities Institute and Intramural Research.

The photograph reprint of André Gide is used by permission and kindness of Mrs. Theodore Steinert. The original is a sanguine by William Rothenstein. Permission to use the 1958 picture of Ernest Hemingway and the marlin has been granted by Von Unruh/Rapho, Paris, France.

GIDE and HEMINGWAY

ABOUT THE AUTHOR

Ben Stoltzfus is Professor of Literature at the University of California, Riverside. He has published articles in the most prestigious literary journals and is also the author of poetry, novels, fiction, and experimental fiction. He has been the recipient of two Fulbright awards to Paris, France, as well as Humanities & Creative Arts Institute awards from the University of California.

INTRODUCTION

Gide and Hemingway: what an odd couple! How could these two writers, so highly suspicious of each other, possibly have anything in common? Gide typifies the French intellectual, while Hemingway typifies the American anti-intellectual. For all of Hemingway's virile posturing, he felt obliged, from time to time, to question the masculinity of alleged or suspected homosexuals. Gide, himself an avowed homosexual, felt no shame or guilt about his *cojones,* but in turn, questioned the values of American writers like Hemingway. Hemingway, the soldier, bull ring afficionado, African hunter, and man of action wrote novels and short stories about death, violence, and safari travels and became a myth during his own lifetime. Gide, though of robust health, eschewed action per se in favor of the more abstract battles of religion and the intellect. Nevertheless, he joined the Communist party, travelled to the USSR, and upon his return, engaged in open polemic with Communist ideology.

In spite of their differences, the influence of both men was enormous. In 1951, the year of Gide's death, Jean-Paul Sartre wrote that "all of French thought in these past thirty years, willing or not, whatever its coordinates may have been elsewhere—Marx, Hegel, Kierkegaard—must also be defined in relation to Gide."[1] As for Hemingway, prose fiction will no doubt forever bear the imprint of his direct, telegraphic, limpid style which draws attention, not to itself, but to the experience behind it. Both men received national and international recognition and were formally honored with the Nobel Prize, Gide in 1947 and Hemingway in 1954.

Considering their differences, notoriety and fame are hardly reasons for tucking Gide and Hemingway under the same covers (the pun is perhaps not unintentional). Difficult as this may seem initially, each author is innovative, rebellious, and original. It is each writer's individual brand of rebellion that interests us, stemming as it seems to, from each one's intimate knowledge of the Bible and the Western cultural tradition. But even here there are difficulties. Hemingway was converted to Catholicism, and at least outwardly, observed many of the conventions of religion, while Gide's "dialogue" with his Catholic opponents revealed a profound mistrust of all forms of institutionalized belief and practice. Underlying their differences, however, are several common sources of inspiration. Both writers exhibit a faith in man and what he can accomplish, an inordinate pride in the will to be human, and a need and desire to fulfill specifically human potentialities. These premises, directly and indirectly, lead both writers to challenge social values, outmoded beliefs, and, as we shall see, God himself.

Even though the discussion of each author's humanistic values implies parallels and oblique comparisons between the two, this study is not, in and of itself, a comparative one. The Gide essay, in addition to a general discussion of his ideas, focuses on *The Notebooks of André Walter* and *Saul*, two early, neglected works in which Gide's persona rebels against God. The Hemingway essay, while dealing primarily with *The Old Man and the Sea*, does so in the larger, general context of his work in relation to Christianity and existentialism. Both studies use the Christian tradition to explicate each author's work and thought. The invisible thread connecting Gide and Hemingway is their need to assert a purely human stamp against the forces of an implacable destiny—a destiny called death. Gide expressed this attitude early in his career, whereas nowhere in Hemingway's work is it more clearly felt than at the end of his career in *The Old Man and the Sea.*

I

Gide
and the Voices of Rebellion

wisdom begins where fear ends . . .
with the revolt of Prometheus.

André Gide
Journal, December 14, 1933

André Gide in 1918 at 49 years of age.

Drawing by William Rothenstein,
reproduced courtesy of Mrs.
Theodore Steinert.

GIDE THE (IM)MORALIST

The Dostoevsky centenary celebration in Paris in 1921 featured, among other events, an allocution at Jacques Copeau's Vieux-Colombier theater by André Gide, the novelist and founder in 1908 of the now famous *Nouvelle Revue Française*. The novel in the Western World, said Gide, "except for very few exceptions, is concerned solely with relationships among men, relationships of passion or intellect, family or society relationships, or those of social classes—but never, almost never, of the individual's relationship with himself or with God."[1]

Although referring to Dostoevsky, Gide was apparently thinking of his own endeavors. What attracted him to the author of *The Possessed,* in spite of Nietzsche's earlier announcement corcerning God's death, were the Russian writer's protagonists' insistent dialogues with themselves, with God, and with Mammon. Gide's books, like Dostoevsky's, describe the battles his heroes and heroines wage with their divided selves. These struggles for identity go hand in glove with Gide's own search for authenticity, or, as he would also say, "sincerity." "The only drama that really interests me and that I would like to relate again and again is the dispute of every individual with whatever prevents him from being authentic, with whatever is opposed to his integrity, to his integration."[2]

Varied as Gide's fiction is, it is self-contained, even coherent, so that from *The Notebooks of André Walter* (1891), through *Saul* (1903), all the way to *Theseus* (1946) we can chart a sinuous, oscillating path stressing bondage, self-deception, spiritual blindness, and submission to authority—forms of inauthenticity that Gide dramatizes in order to move us, his readers, toward insight, creativity, and freedom.

The contrapuntal use of bondage and freedom, within Gide's works, reflects his lifelong effort to define moral good and evil. Whatever inhibits the development of man's authentic being is evil and that which enhances it is good. Hence the exuberance of a book like *Fruits of the Earth* (1897), in which Gide's persona has liberated itself from the bonds that once interfered with its development. The self is free at last to savor earthly instead of heavenly nourishment and it manifests this new-found strength joyously. The opposite of joy is sadness, dejection, and melancholy: "melancholy is merely subsided fervor."[3] We have only to read the *Journal* entries of 1916 accompanying the writing of *Numquid et tu . . . ?* to understand the meaning of this particular juxtaposition. In January and February of 1916 Gide is reading Bossuet and Pascal and praying fervently. One month later he speaks of insomnia, nervous troubles, and his extreme continence. In October, 1916, he refers to a desperate struggle, the dominion of sadness, the diminution of fervor, and a feeling of despair verging on suicide and madness. He speaks of conversion, writes *Numquid et tu . . . ?*, makes soul-shattering entries in his *Journal,* asks for God's help, yet he is also writing *If it Die* (1920). Gide's Catholic critics speak of duplicity. Even if we were to label a demonstration of this kind by so harsh a name it would be impossible not to see a parallel between the coexistence of biographical extremes and their artistic equivalence in his fiction. By October, 1917, Gide has recovered from the "crisis" and by the end of November he basks in an "immense dizzying happiness" (*Journal,* November 30, 1917). Gide concludes that where God has failed, man has triumphed. It is a triumph of joy and the flesh versus austerity and godliness. André Walter, the protagonist of *The Notebooks of André Walter,* followed an opposite path and went mad. Alissa, the heroine of *Strait is the Gate* (1909), died. It is as though Gide were recording the drama of another fictional character, himself, and the *Journal* had become another novel.[4]

Gide spoke frequently of the need to "manifester," to make public, to show, to reveal, or to bear witness to. It is no accident that, in *Le Traité du Narcisse* (1891) the author's persona says: "We live in order to manifest and bring forth. The rules of morality and esthetics are the same: every work of art which does not manifest or bring forth is useless and therefore bad. Every man who does not manifest or bring forth is useless and bad." Gide's *Journal* "reveals" that the processes of art and the processes of living bear such a striking resemblance to each other that one is tempted to agree with Oscar Wilde: life does perhaps imitate art.

In Gide's fiction the moral and the esthetic points of view coincide. Each one of his works, while not always a moral treatise, touches on a moral issue close to Gide. Each one is a fragment of the mosaic. While the Gidian "dialogue" is an artistic device, a juxtaposition of opposites, an esthetic stance inherited from Goethe, it is consubstantial with Gide's desire to "manifest." The form of the dialogue is esthetic but its content is moral.

Many critics have stressed Gide's search for integrity and revolt against external authority, but they have not always analyzed the meaning of this revolt in terms of the rebellious self which, in Gidian terms, triggers the mechanism of self-preservation, i.e., the reaction of an inner, humanistic self versus an outer, authoritarian voice. This striving for authenticity of the inner self against external imperatives raises the issue of "sincerity" which, in Gide's case, is sometimes misinterpreted.[5]

It is misinterpreted because the question of authenticity is so complex. First, there is a fidelity to the self which may require social duplicity. On this level we might, for instance, get the marvelous development of Stendhal's Julien Sorel. Second, there is a fidelity to art, which may be interpreted as insincerity, if a different ethic of allegiance is postulated. Gide's *Journal* falls in this category. Finally, there is self-deception, based perhaps on a fidelity to social, moral or religious values which, on the surface, and because they conform, may appear sincere to others but which, in fact, according to Gide, may deny basic needs. Gide placed Jacques Copeau, Henri Ghéon, Charles Du Bos and all his other converted friends in this category. "There is not one of these conversions in which I do not detect some secret, unavowable motivation; fatigue, fear, disappointment, sickness, sexual or emotional impotence" (*Journal,* December 14, 1933). Gide considered every convert to Catholicism a war casualty suffering from a spiritual trauma comparable to being gassed. "For there is not one of these converted cases whose mind did not reveal some crack (which the least subtle and careful psychological examination always detects) through which the mystical gas was able to penetrate."[6]

Gide maintained that in such cases insincerity parades a mask of religion strong enough to alter the needs of the authentic self, and that the weakened self, as in the case of the *Prodigal* (Gide's version of the *Prodigal Son*), either out of fatigue or laziness or despair, submits to the comfort and reassurance of a preestablished system like the Church or, more frequently these days, to the big brother image of the large corporation. The moment we fall into the strait jacket of ready-made conventions we stop being creative in our moral relationships, or moral in our creative lives, for that matter. Gide viewed authoritarianism or, more specifically, submission to it, as a disease capable of destroying the free, creative spontaneity of the self. The entire question of Gidian sincerity, then, revolves around the issue of the authentic and free self versus the inauthentic self enslaved by an a priori system. Assuming the structure of an authoritarian environment there can be no search for the authentic self without some form of preliminary revolt.*

It has been said: the fear of God is the beginning of wisdom; and then, with God's disappearance, the fear remains. Today it should be understood that wisdom begins where fear ends, with the revolt of Prometheus.
It has been said, you let it be said, that it was first a question of believing. It is first a question of doubting. [*Journal*, December 14, 1933]

Gide insists that the beginning of wisdom is a form of Cartesian doubt. Sincerity then is a point of view. It is subjective (the way I see things) or objective (the way others see me). If I, like Julien Sorel, pay lip service to objective values because my secret ambition must use them temporarily in order to succeed, who is to say that my goal, once achieved, is insincere? Submission or revolt defines what is good for the self and the self either remains faithful to its needs or it succumbs. "They thought I was a rebel (Claudel and Jammes) because I was unable to get—or unwilling to demand—from myself the cowardly submission which would have ensured my comfort" (*Journal*, July 14, 1914).[7]
It is insincere, argues Gide, to submit to an authority which

---

*See Holdheim, p. 15, who believes, as I do, that Gide's work must be situated within the context of his early rebellion, "since Gide's revolt is the point of departure of his entire intellectual adventure."

contradicts the needs of the authentic self. Gide concurs with his Catholic "opponents" that man cannot serve both God and Mammon though, significantly, many of Gide's fictional characters do not know whom they are serving. In *The Pastoral Symphony* (1919) the pastor cannot distinguish between the voice of God and the voice of Mammon. His moral trauma and confusion are so great that he must write a journal in the hope that its narrative will isolate and define the tragic meaning of events which have overwhelmed him.

François Mauriac, though not as vehemently as others, attacked Gide's "reversal" of values and criticized him severely for turning the world "upside down."

No one could have wagered against Christianity with more reasoned detachment and deliberateness than Gide.

Most men choose not to choose. Very few dare decide that evil is good and that good is evil. Very few dare, as Bossuet put it: 'to reverse the tribunal of the conscience which condemned all crimes.' That is what Gide accomplished with a tranquillity, a serenity, a joy which were frightening.[8]

For Gide, the questions of God and Mammon, of good and evil, of right and wrong, were all relative and dependent entirely on the authoritarian-humanistic dichotomy, of the outer vs. the inner-directed person. The Catholics felt it incumbent upon them to attack Gide's system of nondirective, humanistic ethics just as strongly as he was attacking their authoritarian system. Gide's correspondence with Paul Claudel and Francis Jammes represents, basically, the confrontation of these two mutually exclusive "systems."[9]

Gide was not, however, as his Catholic opponents were claiming, rejecting Christian morality. "I know of nothing more important in the history of humanity. I come back to it constantly and I know that there are two teachings whose virtue man will never exhaust: that of Christ, and that of 'Greek fable.' And that Christ's is infinitely superior . . ." (*Journal*, January 23, 1923). Gide was rejecting primarily an a priori system which provided little room for personal initiative and the kind of moral re-creation compatible with each distinct individual. This is why the boy, Gide, in *If it Die* (1920) insists so strongly that he is "not like the others." This is why the question of individuality is treated ironically in *Prometheus Misbound* (1899). This is why, as an amateur botanist, Gide dwells on the specificity and distinct quality of each flower or plant. Gide is almost pathologically afraid that the individuality of man will be smothered under the control of a rigid system which does not provide for differentiation. He wants to preserve the many complexities and possibilities of being. He was not advocating moral anarchy or revolution, though it must have seemed so to many. He was proposing, long before Sartre was, that every man, insofar as he was intelligent enough to do so, act according to values which would constantly be questioned, reevaluated and re-created.

Gide's authorial point of view *is* critical and ironic: it is critical of submission to authority; it is critical of excess; it is critical of duplicity and blindness (moral as well as spiritual); and it is critical of diseased individualism. Gide fought against the complacency and smugness of militant a priori systems.

Actually, the totality of Gide's work is a treatise on morals. The irony in his "dialogue" with the Catholic Church is that he saw the devil working through the Church while the Church accused him of being the devil. Jean Anouilh's treatment of Joan of Arc in *L'Alouette* presents a parallel study of such a conflict. The Inquisition is accusing Joan of heresy and individualism. She must recant. But in order to do so she must renounce the meaning of her inner voices, in other words, deny the very essence of her being—her integrity. This she refuses to do and she is burned because she protested against the authority of the Mother Church. Gide too would defend the authenticity of inner voices, particularly if they oppose the structure of some external monolith. But he was acutely aware that crass self-ishness, as in the case of *The Immoralist* (1902), may violate the delicate balance of human relationships. He stressed the importance of reason and the reasoned evaluation of a choice, an act, or an event. In such a context his flirtation with and rejection of Communism was an example of intellect rectifying an error prompted by desire. "I had to recognize my error, and that it was Christian virtues I hoped to find in Communism" (*Journal*, July 14, 1941).

The irony of this statement is surely not unintentional, the implication being that although Christian virtues are not outdated, the Church is. "Oh! everything would be fine if one had only Christ to deal with! But religion is not Christ; it is the priest" (*Journal* July 1, 1931). Communism was indeed, as Raymond Aron has noted, the opiate of many intellectuals who, disillusioned with the forms of Western Christianity as well as capitalism, looked to communism with unabashedly starry eyes. Gide, unlike most, was quickly disillusioned. Though he liked the Russian people he recognized that a political dictatorship tyrannized the individual as much, though in a different way, as any moral dictatorship. He spoke of Christianity as "that incomparable school of individualization, in which each is more precious than all" (*Journal*, May 25, 1940). That he looked toward communism for such individualism presupposes that, either he knew nothing about Stalinism, or, as is quite probable, he wanted to exploit the additional possibilities for "dialogue" within the political arena. By 1937 he virtually equates communism with fascism: "The historians of tomorrow will examine how and why, the end being effaced by the means, the Communist spirit ceased to be opposed to the Fascist spirit, and even to be differentiated from it" (*Journal*, August 5, 1937).[10]

Gide's emphasis on ends and means is not surprising. *Fruits of the Earth* (1897) shouts the fact that living is an end in itself, not a means for the future satisfactions that communism's distant historical paradise might promise. There is too much of an amused, self-indulgent Pan in Gide to take the ponderous rhetoric of communism seriously. Naturally, he relegates communism to those evil doctrinaire systems, along with fascism, Hitlerism, and Catholicism, which stifle either the political, the social, or the moral fiber of man. Gide insists that an unquestioning, unreasoned submission to the spiritual authority and control of the Church (Protestant or Catholic) is as dangerous as the submission to Hitlerism (*Journal*, July 1, 1942). While he expected much from the ideology of Marxist teachings, the harsh authoritarianism of the Stalin regime was an anathema to him. It is understandable that the suppression of individual freedom in Russia for the sake of remote historical goals would have displeased Gide as much as the encroachments of the Church on any one person's spiritual self-determination.[11]

Because of the unequivocal nature of his stand Gide has been attacked and defended with equal fervor. For his adversaries he was the incarnation of the devil, while for his defenders he was virtue personified. For those hostile to him he was a vicious and degrading influence, while the people who liked him, heralded the liberating forces of his thought. One side saw him as a corrupter of youth and tradition, while the other side, comparing him to Socrates, stressed the grandeur and necessity of this corruption. Indeed, rather than accept doctrine, or the status quo, and for the sake of spontaneity and freedom, Gide was forever rebelling against the gods of convention. Like Prometheus stealing the fire from Jupiter, Gide fought against authoritarian systems and values in an attempt to give man an awareness of his truly human potential.

Unlike Socrates, Gide died of old age at eighty-two. There was poison, to be sure, distilled from the pens of critics like Henri Massis and Henri Béraud, but instead of hurting him, such studies as "La Confession d'André Gide," or "La Défaite d'André Gide" (published by Massis along with other essays in 1948 under the title *D'André Gide à Marcel Proust*, Paris: Lardanchet) enhanced his literary career and helped to make his reputation. The more his opponents attacked him the more Gide thrived on their assaults. It was as though their confrontation served to sharpen the tips of his own arrows. The challenge made it possible for him to define himself more fully.

The strange thing, when speaking of *influence*, is that one almost always considers only direct influences. Influence through protest is, in certain natures, at least as important; it is at times much more so, yet most often very difficult to recognize. It is by no means always through affection, weakness and the need for imitation that our characters are bent. A comparatively strong nature yields more to reaction than to direct action. The opponents interest me more than the followers.[12]

Like an athlete who thrives on competition and discipline, the "moral opposition" helped to maintain the artistic balance and tension of Gide's work.

I do not mean to suggest that Gide always liked what was said about him. On the contrary, his pride and vision of himself as an artist, as his *Journal* reveals, were often piqued by the insults. "Massis never retains from a writing but what can serve his thesis. He is one of the most dishonest minds that I know, for whom everything is fuel when he wants to burn someone else" (*Journal*, February 11, 1941). Inevitably, behind the attacks on Gide, there lurked a moral tone, a condemnation in the name of inalienable dogma. Gide used such criticism as a springboard from which to bounce back and through which to affirm himself. "Moreover, these protests, more than anything, have given me assurance of my reality, of my value; or even,

more precisely: they themselves brought these qualities in me to light"
(*Journal*, January 30, 1931).

Gide's Catholic critics formed one of the backdrops in his
"dialogue." Like Prometheus feeding his eagle, Gide cultivated one
opponent after another (himself, even God), so that, in the end, he
might slay the eagle and with each feather write a work of art.

Nevertheless, each work of art was a part of the whole, a fragment
of the mosaic whose moral purpose was to challenge external authority
in order to proclaim the virtues of the inner-directed man. God, as one
of the authority figures (in addition to the Church, the State, and the
Family), received more than his share of Gide's attacks. "Faith moves
mountains," said Gide, "yes: mountains of absurdities."[13] The Church,
understandably, attacked him for such "blasphemy." In *Numquid*
(1916), in his *Dostoevsky* (1923), and in the *New Fruits of the Earth*
(1935), Gide insisted that man's salvation on earth did not depend on
God, nor on fate, nor on an afterlife. Gide emphasized self-fulfillment
through creative self-discipline. Only the sustained discipline of the
inner-directed man, he argued, would effect the kind of change in
human relationships which could be viewed as "progress:"

Cannot man learn to demand of himself, through virtue, what he thinks
is demanded by God? He must nevertheless manage to; at least some
must, to start with; otherwise the game would be up. This strange
game that we are playing on earth (unwittingly, unknowingly, and
often unwillingly) will be won only if the idea of God, as it recedes,
yields to virtue; only if man's virtue and dignity supersedes and supplants God. God has ceased to exist except by virtue of man. *Et eritis
sicut dei.* (It is thus that I wish to understand that old word of the
Tempter—who, like God, exists only in our minds—and to see in this
offer, which we have been told is fallacious, a possibility of salvation.)[14]

Gide believed that man could effect his own salvation without God,
that God was an idea or an ideal that could be defined to suit man's
needs or goals. Consequently God is always in the process of becoming.
He is in the future and his existence is entirely dependent on man:
"Man is responsible for God," said Gide (*Journal*, April 10, 1942).[15]

From the moment that I understood that God was not yet, but was
becoming, and that he depended on each one of us for his becoming,
my own moral sense was restored. No impiety, no presumption in this

thought; for I was convinced that God was achieved only by man and through man at the same time; nevertheless, if man led to God, creation, in order to lead to man, started from God; so that the divine could be found at both ends, at the start and at the point of arrival, and that the start was there in order to take man to God. This double-valved thought reassured me and I was no longer willing to dissociate one from the other: God creating man in order to be created by him; God the end of man; chaos raised up by God to man's level, and then man raising himself up to God's level. To admit only one of them: what fear, what obligation! To admit only the other: what conceit! It was no longer a matter of obeying God, but of making him come alive, of falling in love with him, of demanding him for oneself out of love and by getting him through virtue. [*Journal,* June 3-7, 1942]

Gide was saying, in essence, that man is capable of creating an ideal morality named God. It is less clear what Gide meant by a creation that began with God. This original God, in the natural order of things, would have to precede the second, since God is behind a creation which engenders man, who in turn creates God. The first God, a throwback perhaps to Voltaire's deism, seems to be a naturalistic one whom Gide identifies with the Universe and its creative force—God, the clockmaker, who sets the world in motion. This motion, which Gide seems to define as evolution, finally created a being called man. The second God is created by man. Man projects a certain moral perfectibility onto the screen of future history, calls it God, and then strives to fulfill this vision of an ideal world.*

If we interpret Nietzsche's "death of God" as meaning that there will be no future significant biological changes (evolution) in man, then in order to live again, God, envisioned as a process of human perfectibility on the moral level, has to be re-created. Biologists like Julian Huxley define this process as the future social evolution of man. Gide would have concurred. Hence Gide's emphasis on movement and constant change. Immobility, he said, leads to moral and spiritual atrophy and, eventually, to the tyranny of dogma.

Gide objected to the stasis and complacency of faith and dogma which offered man consolation, assurance and comfort; where everything was set up to protect his laziness and to shelter the mind from

---

*For a liberal Protestant evaluation of Gide's views and definition of God, see H. J. Nersoyan, *André Gide: The Theism of an Atheist.*

effort (*Journal,* July 1, 1942). In 1907 he wrote his own version of *The Return of the Prodigal Son* in which the prodigal's return is due not to faith, but to weakness, laziness, and corruption. He has squandered a fortune in pursuit of pleasure, and now, unable to adapt to the world, he seeks the security and comfort of his Father's house. He returns, confessing his failure, hoping that the youngest brother, unhindered and unfettered, will be able to make his way unaided in the difficult world beyond the walls. In Gide's variant of the biblical parable, the Father, as in the original, is the analogue for God, the House is the Church, and faith the necessary prelude to salvation. Gide, however, turns the tables. To return to the House of the Lord is to admit failure, whereas to survive beyond the walls is a manifestation of strength, courage, independence, and self-sufficiency. The Church, says Gide, is for the weak. The world is for the strong. Faith is for those who feel inadequate, for those who can't do. To envisage an ideal moral order, called God, and to strive to create it, is for the strong.

Man's ability to stand on his "own two feet," in contrast to the Prodigal's inability to do so, is an example Gide draws on for the progression of mankind.

Little Edith Heurgon is beginning to walk. Never before have I witnessed anything so marvelous: the first steps of a small child. Having been held until now, all of a sudden it begins to understand that it can stand up without support, go forth alone ... Humanity has scarcely reached this stage, still tottering, dizzied by the space yet to be covered, atilt, incompletely weaned from the milk of beliefs. [*Journal,* July 15, 1943]

Gide would have liked to see man stand alone, unaided and unafraid. It is the rebels, he says, who will save the world, if indeed the world is going to be saved. Those who submit to the tyranny of the mind will, consciously or unconsciously, prevent man's emancipation.

Worn out by yesterday's struggle, young men (and a number of their elders) look for and think that they find, in this very submission, rest, assurance, and intellectual comfort. Why, they even seek in it a reason for living and convince themselves (or let themselves be convinced) that they will be of better service and will take on their full value, when enlisted to do so. Thus it is that, without really realizing it, or realizing it only too late, through obedience or laziness, they are going to contribute to the defeat, the ruin of the spirit.[16]

THE NOTEBOOKS OF ANDRÉ WALTER

Gide believed fervently that the rebels would inherit the earth, that the Kingdom of God would belong to those who doubt. Nevertheless, as a young man, up to approximately 1893, he was neither a rebel nor a doubter. During his early manhood he was trying to resolve the strict Puritan code of his mother's Protestant teachings with the lure of an imperious sexuality. He projected this moral drama onto his fictional characters who were struggling with their "consciences" in an attempt to harmonize the two sides of their split identities.

The voices of God or of Mammon, as the voices of conscience with which Gide's characters are wrestling, lead them, on the one hand, away from insight and, on the other, toward an integration of self. In their search for authenticity, Gide's protagonists hear a variety of voices, be they the voice of the devil, as in *Saul* (1903), the internalized voice of God and religion, as in *Strait is the Gate* (1909), the collective voice of patriotism and society, as in *Philoctetes* (1899), the male chauvinist voice of the father, as in *Genevieve* (1936). The protagonist's ability or inability to resolve the conflicts engendered by the contradictory voices coming from within and impinging from without, constitute Gide's artistic "dialogue."

In pursuing this dialogue, Gide frequently emphasized the overlapping between life and art. Each of his books is an exaggeration of inherent possibilities which, once realized in fiction, will not be duplicated in life, at least not by Gide. He has insisted that a work of art is like the flowering of a rosebud, the bringing to fruition of desire which is then discarded in the process of creation.

How many buds we carry within us . . . which will blossom only in our books! . . . But if we wilfully snuff out all *but one*, how quickly it will develop and grow! . . . My recipe for creating a hero is very simple: take one of these buds, put it in a pot—all by itself—soon you will have a marvelous individual. Advice: choose preferably (if indeed you have a choice) the bud which bothers you the most. You can rid yourself of it in the process.[1]

While specific dramas in Gide's life seem to explain the genesis of certain works, Gide's life as a whole balances his fiction. The reasoned actions of his life counteract the "rosebuds" of his characters, Gide rejected Alissa's "mistakes" in *Strait is the Gate* (1909) just as surely as he rejected Michel's "excesses" in *The Immoralist* (1902).

The exaggerated behavior of Michel and Alissa, the monstrous rosebuds of their personalities, have all the effects of a distorting mirror. But the distortion is moral rather than physical. We are no doubt familiar with mirrors capable of making us look tall or short, fat or slim, yet in spite of the deformation, we perceive the resemblance and recognize possibilities which, although they may not be our own, operate within the realm of experience. Each one of Gide's works is a philosophical mirror and his art a gallery of reflections. Like the pieces of glass and the mosaic patterns of the kaleidoscope Gide talks of at some length in his book *If it Die* (1920), the multiple composition shifts, blends, reforms itself, and is forever changing—a transformation that is dependent on the evolving configurations of each agglomeration. In contrast to the toy kaleidoscope the youthful André broke deliberately one day, in order to fathom and expose its mysteries, we run no risk of ruining Gide's art by dissecting it and analyzing its components.

Nevertheless, the constant metamorphoses of the colored bits of glass suggest the complexity of Gide's work and the difficulties of exegesis, particularly when his life and art overlap in such strange and unexpected ways. Moreover, Gide's insistence on an inherent duality in life and art, his frequent allusions to a state of dialogue within himself, authorize us to structure a framework of extremes within which all possibilities are relevant. Beyond *The Vatican Swindle* (1914) and the ironic humor of his farcical novel (Gide called it a *sotie*) we catch glimpses of an adult Gide who describes himself as a little boy having fun under the watchful and annoying gaze of a Protestant minister (*Journal*, June 22, 1907).

While Gide took particular pleasure in noting and recording all events, facts, and phenomena that would enhance the idea of opposition and duality, some of these are more important than others. He specifically capitalized on the possibilities for dialogue between his Catholic and Protestant backgrounds. His now celebrated exchange with Maurice Barrès over being "rooted" or "uprooted" served in part to accentuate the knowledge that Gide himself, while born in Paris, came from two distinct backgrounds and two different geographical areas in France: "Is it *my* fault if your God took such great care to have me born under two different stars, the product of two separate races, two provinces, and two religions?" (*Journal*, December 2, 1929). He observes, not without humor and without believing in astrology, that on November 21, his birthday, the earth leaves the influence of Scorpio to enter the phase of Sagittarius.

At other times Gide alludes to the beautiful equilibrium of French culture as a product of a historical confrontation of extremes—among them the opposition of Pascal and Montaigne or of Claudel and Valéry—of faith versus scepticism. "I feel I am a product of French culture; attached to it by all the forces of my heart and of my mind. I cannot distance myself from this culture without losing sight of myself, without ceasing to be myself" (*Journal*, February 13, 1943). With most of his work already written, Gide was perhaps justified, in 1943, in flattering himself so brazenly. While his *Journal* is peppered with egotistical references, many statements concerning his duality also stress the two main influences on French culture. A 1931 *Journal* entry reads as follows: "The Christian ideal . . . yes; but the Greco-Latin ideal has played an equally important part . . . in making us what we are. Most astonishing is that people have tried to bring together, even blend, these very different *influences* into one single 'tradition'" (March 17).

Gide repeatedly drew his inspiration, his subject matter, his characters, and the titles of his works from Greek mythology and the Bible: Oedipus, Theseus, Philoctetes, Saul, Bathsheba, the Prodigal Son. Each one of these characters is also the title of a work, while in *Prometheus Misbound* (1899), instead of opposing the separate traditions, Gide blends them into one narrative whole. A Gide-Prometheus, in rebellion against God, manages to place himself at the center of the cultural opposition, thus conveying the impression that *he* is the living synthesis of an artistic and cultural dichotomy.[2] This is typical of Gide's mercurial nature, the duality itself forming an esthetic constant. However, the moment he achieves a union of opposites he uses the new-found harmony as a springboard for yet another confrontation. "It will not be easy to trace the trajectory of my mind; its slant will reveal itself only in my style and will frequently escape notice. If, based on my latest work, someone thinks he has at last seized my resemblance, let him beware: it is from my last born that I am always the most different."[3]

More than anything, it is Gide's play of antitheses which reminds us of Victor Hugo who blends good and evil, light and dark, love and death, the grotesque and the sublime, the beautiful and the ugly. However, Gide's complexity, unlike Hugo's, derives not from the fusion of multiple elements into one work, but from the repetition of a few basic themes throughout his many works.[4] Since Gide was weaned on the Bible it is perhaps unavoidable that his books should communicate some of the Bible's dramatic sense, emphasizing as it does the confrontation of good and evil, body and soul, salvation and damnation. In 1893 Gide wrote:

The essence of a Christian soul is to imagine its own battles; after a while it no longer understands why . . . Since, in the end, whoever is the loser, it is always a part of oneself; but the wear and tear is unnecessary. I spent my whole youth opposing these two selves within me, when perhaps they would have preferred to get along. Out of a love of combat I imagined many struggles and divided my natural self.[5]

Gide's first novel, *The Notebooks of André Walter* (1891), antici-pating by two years the *Journal* entry quoted above, describes the struggle for supremacy between the protagonist's two *natural* yet *embattled* selves. In March, 1889 a fictitious André Walter goes to Brittany to write a novel called *Allain* which, he says, will be a "strange, scientific, and passionate" book. Ten months later André Walter dies mad, leaving his novel and his journal to posterity. These notebooks, from which the work derives its title, are the notes for his journal, a book in two parts, the "white" and the "black," written allegedly by André Walter about Allain whose name, initially, was to have graced André Gide's title page.

Considering the volumes that have been written on Gide's life and works, there is, relatively speaking, very little in print concerning *The Notebooks of André Walter*. Exegesis, more often than not, is a form of biographical criticism with emphasis, by the majority of commentators, on Gide's use of *The Notebooks* to persuade his cousin Madeleine to marry him. This she refused to do until after the death of Mme. Gide, a refusal for which Madeleine is sometimes quoted as saying that it was not death that she feared, but marriage.

Intriguing as Gide's lifetime relationship to Madeleine may have been (and it is intriguing), the anecdotal and biographical approach to literature, specifically to *The Notebooks,* does limit perception of the work's esthetic and structural dimensions. Jean Delay's analysis of "the double" at least has the advantage of using biographical material in a psychoanalytic context.[6] On the critical level, Claude Martin gives *The Notebooks* naturalistic dimensions reminiscent of Zola,[7] while Pierre de Boisdeffre believes that *The Notebooks* are an apology for Platonic love.[8] Even though Platonic love seems to have been Gide's intent in offering his first inscribed copy of the book to Madeleine, a work of art is, fortunately, always more than the author's avowed intentions. It is probably fair to say that the structural and social resonance of art will always be greater or lesser than the author intended.

In addition to biographical elements, the German influence, most specifically Goethe's, is also to be felt in Gide's first work—with obvious parallels to be drawn between Werther and Walter. Catherine Savage and Van Meter Ames, in their studies of *The Notebooks,* offer valuable commentaries from literary and ironic points of view.[9] Vinio Rossi, more than other commentators, gives an esthetic evaluation of *The Notebooks* which, fortunately, goes beyond the traditional biographical exegesis of this work and demonstrates that Gide was more concerned with the artistic and psychological mechanisms within himself than with the interplay between himself and Madeleine.[10] It may be useful therefore, considering the record, in order to determine the extent of Gide's incipient revolt in his early works, to situate *The Notebooks* within a humanistic-authoritarian dichotomy, particularly with Van Meter Ames's ironic juxtapositions in mind.[11]

However, before commenting in detail on additional internal evidence for esthetics, irony, and revolt, *The Notebooks of André Walter* probably do not, as Denis de Rougemont claims, represent a secret, mystical longing on Gide's part for the supernatural. Gide's *Journal,* as we have seen, gives us the direction of his moral, ethical, and religious thought which is strictly humanistic and about which there can be no doubt. The swing of the pendulum of his intellect and emotions, back and forth, is a deliberate manifestation of a reasoned dialectic which he explores and exploits in purely artistic terms. Gide's fictional characters can, as Rougemont demonstrates so nicely, be situated within a Tristan-Don Juan opposition, but to suggest that Gide's homosexuality was the necessary obstacle to sleeping with his wife Madeleine, because he and she, after their death, had better things to do in heaven, as an idea, if nothing else, is at least striking by its audacity.

On the mythical level, in keeping with Rougemont's analysis, *The Notebooks of André Walter,* like *Strait is the Gate,* represent the swing of the pendulum toward the Tristan side, while *Fruits of the Earth,* and *The Immoralist,* are the swing of the pendulum toward Don Juanism.[12] What interests us here, however, is not the dialectical process itself, but the relation of Walter's and Allain's abnegation of life with Gide's rebellion against authority, specifically God's.

The Notebooks of André Walter do not have the incisive irony of the *récit* (Gide's word for a novella), the comical exaggeration of the *sotie* (a farcical novella), or the critical acumen of a long novel like *The Counterfeiters.* The themes which will later become Gide's stock-in-trade are, in *The Notebooks,* juxtaposed without distinction. States of mind are described in great detail, dreams are recorded, and the progression of madness is exposed. Although Walter's renunciation of marriage and the world resembles Alissa's abnegation, the consistent brilliance of *Strait is the Gate* reveals itself in flashes only. Additional similarities between *The Notebooks* and *Strait is the Gate* show Walter obeying his mother as Alissa obeys the voice of God. Walter rationalizes his loss of Emmanuèle (the name itself means "one with God") by saying: "Since I must lose her, may I at least find Thee again, O Lord. Bless me for following the strait and narrow path."[13] Alissa's obedience to God is one of the preconditions for her rejection of Jérôme while Walter finds in God a substitute for his love of Emmanuèle—a Gidian irony considering the meaning of her name.

The separation of the flesh and the spirit is also present in both novels. Alissa's asceticism, her rejection of the world, and her progressive withdrawal from it are obsessions that also haunt Walter.

"Bodies hindered me; they hid the souls. *The flesh is useless.* An embrace should be immaterial" (p. 50).

The Tristan myth is predicated on the survival of love in death and on the reality of the soul's afterlife. Gide not only rejected the concept of a "church God," his entire "dialogue" with Catholic proselytizers like Paul Claudel, Francis Jammes, and Charles Du Bos assumes that life is not a means to an end, but is an end in itself. Gide's *Fruits of the Earth*, like Albert Camus's *Nuptials*, stresses the beauties and pleasures of man's "honeymoon" on earth. What mattered ultimately for Gide was not the possibility of union in an afterlife, but the possibilities for self-fulfillment here and now. Gide's life and the message of his works are opposed to the Tristan myth because Gide's values contradict the myth's essential premises.

Gide's early dialogue with and rebellion against God is perhaps best explained, not in terms of the Tristan-Don Juan dichotomy, but in terms of Erich Fromm's ethical and structural dialectic of the Humanistic and Authoritarian consciences. Conscience, says Fromm, is an inner "voice" which makes us feel "good" or "bad" depending on whether we have obeyed or disobeyed it. The Authoritarian conscience speaks for God, the Church, or the Family, while the Humanistic conscience speaks for the self and comes only from the self. The Authoritarian conscience is "the voice of an internalized external authority, the parents, the state, or whoever the authorities in a culture happen to be."[14] The Humanistic conscience, in contrast to the Authoritarian, is not the internalized voice of an authority we might be eager to please and afraid of displeasing, but an inner voice independent of external sanctions and rewards.[15] The Humanistic conscience is the voice of an inner self which prompts man to live productively, fully, and harmoniously in the direction of the self's true potential. It guards the integrity of the self and protects it from Authoritarian voices which might be doing violence to it.

On a purely artistic level Gide metamorphoses the conflict of his two consciences and his two selves into such masterpieces as *The Immoralist* and *Strait is the Gate*. *The Immoralist* is the drama of Michel's contaminated Humanistic conscience which feels responsible only to the needs of the self (the postulate of the Humanistic conscience being precisely this kind of responsibility), while Alissa's drama in *Strait is the Gate* lies not in being responsible to herself (since she loves Jérôme) but in remaining faithful to the voice of God. She suppresses her inner voice, which says "marry Jérôme," and listens instead to the Authoritarian voice of her religion which tells her that, to enter heaven via "the strait gate," she must negate this life and reject Jérôme in order to be worthy of the next.

In *The Immoralist* Gide explores Michel's attempts to free himself from the tyranny of an Authoritarian conscience which has been interfering with the self's inner desire to live fully and harmoniously. The stifling of his Humanistic conscience has produced a sickly and dependent being.

Having, in the course of his African voyage, discovered the meaning of death and life, Michel, in the name of spontaneity, sincerity, and self-fulfillment now severs all ties with his "authoritarian" past in a passionate and desperate effort to free himself. In his struggle for life against death, Michel channels his hostility. He rejects prayer, his wife Marceline's pious invocations, and God's help because, he says, he does not want to be indebted to anyone, not even to God. This exclusive responsibility of the ego to itself is expressed in terms of an animal vitality, in terms of a biological need for survival which leaves no room or time for moral growth. Paralleling Michel's physical recovery is not only a discovery of beauty and life but a new and acute consciousness of death. It is this existential awareness of death which, as it does for the heroes of Sartre and Camus, now activates Michel's appreciation of life.

The psychological verisimilitude of *The Immoralist,* even to the detail of father plagiarizing the work of his son, contributes to and explains the origins as well as the step-by-step progression of Michel's moral philosophy. What matters is the present. The past is identified with the "immobility of death." Michel's erudition interferes with his joy. And so, in a typical succession of antiromantic statements, Michel says that he hates death, ruins, and melancholy. He has the feeling, at last, that he has discovered an authentic being—an inner core which books, teachers, parents, and even he himself had, at first, tried to suppress.

If *The Immoralist* represents the exaggerated voice of the Humanistic conscience, *Strait is the Gate* and *Numquid et tu . . . ?* explore the effects of an exaggerated Authoritarian conscience. Before 1917 Gide seems to have balanced the voices of his two selves, moving alternately from one to the other. After 1917 his value system reinforces the Humanistic conscience, and virtually extinguishes the anxieties of his earlier asceticism. Until that time Gide's Authoritarian and Humanistic consciences seem to have coexisted. First one would gain the upper hand and then the other. Gide's novels and plays, as well as his *Journal*, are the record of the alternating sequence of this phenomenon. It is these swings of the artistic pendulum which, in part, justify the Tristan-Don Juan rapprochement, but which, I believe, are best explained in terms of Fromm's structuralist dichotomy.

The interesting aspect in *The Notebooks of André Walter* (since the above was a necessary, illustrative digression), in addition to the fact that the two voices of conscience coexist, is that in order to please his mother's authoritarianism (that he not marry Emmanuèle) and while taking refuge in God, Walter suppresses his sexuality. If the Tristan myth is to work, T.'s marriage to Emmanuèle in life means that he, T., will lose her in death. So the purpose of Walter's continence is to keep him pure for Emmanuèle. In *The Black Notebook* he, like Jacob, wrestles with his angel. However, in trying to suppress his sexuality, and in his attempt to be worthy of Emmanuèle, he goes mad. If we assume that those who are mad are nearer the angels then, somehow, the struggle has been worth it, but if, on the contrary, we look upon insanity as the result of conflict, frustration, rejection, and all the other complex, intricate, and as yet not fully understood factors which contribute to the alienation of the self, then insanity, though a solution of some kind, is an escape from too harsh a reality into a dream world of fantasy where reality is made to order and where fears, anxieties, and unbearable tensions can, at last, be eliminated.

Walter's dream world, with which he contaminates Allain's, indicates how hard it is for both to follow the "strait road" toward "salvation." Walter is using his life as a means to merit Emmanuèle in death. Allain, like Alissa, says: "I must deserve you by leaving you" (p. 61), or, "Only the Spirit is undying, the flesh is useless."[16] These statements are evidence of the willful suppression of a physical and sensory dimension. Walter exults in "the flesh humiliated by the triumphant soul" (p. 130); "treat your flesh harshly" (p. 137); "you will not conquer unless you do violence to yourself" (p. 137). Walter's notes for August 23 describe the same kind of physical torture Paul Claudel inflicts on the protagonists of his plays. The flesh is humiliated, mutilated, subjugated, and finally vanquished so that the soul, freed of its earthly prison, may fly upward toward God: "What does it matter! This struggle in the darkness is sublime—person to person, body to body . . .

and occasionally, after the victories, pride breathes arrogant raptures upon me. When this struggle does not prostrate me, it is strangely edifying; it is the supreme test which either consumes or exalts" (p. 137).

Nevertheless, Walter is not without his doubts about the final outcome of the struggle. He suspects that in order to have the soul triumph over the body "madness is at the other end" (p. 129); that chastity is perhaps not an exalted state of mind: "Yes vanity, chastity! Vanity is pride disguised" (p. 180). Like Alissa, Walter asks God to deliver him quickly before he blasphemes (p. 181).

In *The Notebooks of André Walter* Gide seems to be working against forces that frustrate the self but, as yet, are not clearly defined. The clear-cut opposition of values in such complementary works as *The Immoralist* and *Strait is the Gate* has not been realized. Walter, as such, is Gide, the incipient artist who has not resolved the con- tradictions of the Authoritarian and the Humanistic conscience. Walter's madness and death are an indication of the road Gide will *not* follow, since Gide's future work will reveal a progressive orienta- tion to and acceptance of life.

Jacob wrestling with the angel will be one of the Gidian metaphors for man's dialogue with God, or the devil. In fact, Walter's description of the two adversaries, the angel and the beast, the soul and the flesh, also defines Gide's artistic use and confrontation of extremes. Alissa of *Strait is the Gate* will represent the soul while Michel of *The Immoralist* is the flesh. While Gide supports neither extreme, their symbolic opposition is one phase of his moral and esthetic dialogue.

Amorphous as the *Notebooks* are, they do have a certain irony. *The Black Notebook* begins with the Latin epigraph: "Pro remedio animae meae . . ." a tacit recognition that since Emmanuèle has been "lost" there is now much to be done. As the novel Walter is writing blends more and more with his own daydreams, the epitaph he writes for Allain is not without humor:

> Here lies Allain who went mad
> Because he thought he had a soul. [p. 172]

One could argue, I suppose, that madness, as an escape from too harsh a reality substitutes a happiness of its own for a previous set of unbearable conditions. But I wonder if "mad happiness," even if it did exist, does not represent an impasse, an impotent state of affairs. Reason can indicate, to those capable of reason, what they should do to fulfill themselves. This active fulfillment of the self which Spinoza also calls the "good" is accompanied, as a by-product, by happiness. The corollary is that a frustrated person becomes unhappy and depressed. If this unhappiness is extreme enough to produce a break with reality (suicide would be an extreme example) then we say that a person has gone insane. Walter's hallucination of a resurrected Emmanuèle would in effect be such a dead-end happiness. I see no reason to suppose that his vision of Emmanuèle does not make him happy, but such happiness is a snare, a trap from which he cannot escape and which, in his case, leads to suicide.

Walter's suicide represents an answer which Gide rejects. Each of Gide's subsequent works will be an experimental solution to different aspects of the same problem: how can a person fulfill himself in freedom and what happens to him if and when he submits to the tyranny of authoritarian values? From this question emerge parallel questions and considerations such as: What is freedom? (treated in *The Immoralist*, 1902); Is there such a thing as a gratuitous act? (treated in *The Vatican Swindle*, 1914); Is conscience reliable? (treated in *The Pastoral Symphony*, 1919); etc. Each of Gide's works is a variation on these basic themes. The fact that few Gidian characters, perhaps only Theseus, achieve an ideal state of equilibrium is no indication that Gide had not resolved the conflicting tendencies within himself before he published *Theseus* (1946). Gide's fiction is a working out of problematic difficulties and his characters never achieve the lucidity he does.

Walter's asceticism leads to madness, and suicide. Gide uses him in order to defend the human against the antihuman. The "good" exalts man and the "bad" debases him. Walter's behavior and Alissa's behavior suppress the human for the sake of the divine. Walter and Alissa want to please God and, in the process destroy themselves. To destroy characters who are subservient to God corresponds to a rebellion which, conscious or not, Gide directs against God's authoritarian and puritanical voice. Gide's Saul, unlike Walter and Alissa, as we shall see, strives for fulfillment, not by submitting to God's will, but by opposing it.

SAUL

On July 15, 1931, ten years after the Dostoevsky allocution at the Vieux-Colombier and twenty-eight years after Gide had published his play *Saul* (1903), he made the following notation in his *Journal:* "Upon rereading my play it seems to me to be one of the best things I have written, and perhaps the most surprising. It will be discovered some day and people will probably be astonished that it could have remained unknown for so long."* This play is surprising because it contains the very essence of the now familiar Gidian elements—among them his dialogue with God—in a form so pure as to belie attention. Not until *The Counterfeiters* (1926) will Gide be able again to combine the tension and complexity of multiple elements in one work of art. It is certainly true, as many commentators have already observed, that *The Notebooks of André Walter* contain all or most of Gide: *The White Notebook* and *The Black Notebook* are seen to represent the two antagonistic poles of his personality which will in turn create the "dialogue"; there is also the exaggeration of a personality trait which, like Alissa's asceticism, will lead the hero of the *Notebooks* to madness and suicide; *André Walter* also contains the oblique point of view, the journal within the journal and a certain deliberate posturing, all typical of Gide's work. Though the reader may easily discern these

---

*In 1920 Roger Martin du Gard told Gide that if he had to choose *one* of Gide's works to take with him to a deserted island he would choose *Saul*. *Notes sur André Gide*, p. 31.

Gidian elements, the work itself is flawed. What makes *Saul* so interesting by contrast is that it too contains most of the Gidian ingredients but combined in a viable artistic form.

Jean Hytier calls *Saul* a "magnificent drama," and like R.-M. Albérès, Claude Martin, and Jean-Jacques Thierry, he sees the play as a failure of the will, the demise of action, the dissolution of a man who surrenders to all his desires.[1] These commentators refer to a passage in Gide's *Journal* (April 28, 1943) in which Gide describes a chrysalis with the incipient shape of a perfect butterfly that has been devoured from within by parasites. Gide himself compares this chrysalis to Saul who is "consumed" by the demons of desire.

Convincing as such an exegesis is, it also leaves room for additional commentary that allows us to focus on Saul's, and also by implication, on Gide's "rebellion." In this context, the dialogue between Saul and God and the dialogue between Saul and David are a dramatization of Gide's internal conflicts—a confrontation between Fromm's Authoritarian and Humanistic consciences. If Saul is immobilized and his will paralyzed, it is because of the contradictory and mutually exclusive voices of Samuel and the devils. Samuel's ghost is the authoritarian voice speaking for God, society, and the family. He is the reincarnation of Freud's superego, while the devils are the id, representing desire—the humanistic self purged of the dictates of God.

Saul is "surprising," therefore, because it contains, in germ form, the essence of Gide's psychological and artistic drama, not only because the polarization typical of *The Immoralist* and *Strait is the Gate* exists within the same work, but also because this play portrays Saul as an incipient homosexual. Since Gide considered *Corydon* (written in 1916, but published in 1924) his most significant work (Gide was perhaps the first important writer of the twentieth century to discuss homosexuality openly), this central preoccupation of his, as yet unresolved, finds itself expressed artistically in the five acts of Saul's drama. Saul, in his conversation with the shadow of the dead prophet Samuel, asks what his original mistake was and is informed that he should never have welcomed David.

Saul. But since God had chosen him.
Samuel. Do you think that God, in order to punish you, had not already foreseen the latest vacillations of your soul? He has placed your enemies before the gate; they hold your punishment in their hands;

behind your half-closed door, they are waiting; but they have been summoned now for a long time. You too feel in your heart these impatient expectations: you know very well that what you call fear is really desire.[2]

Samuel's statement is accurate enough, since the person Saul both loves and fears is David.

Are we to assume that because Saul is a homosexual Gide tried to purge himself of this particular brand of sexuality? Since Gide did not reject uranism, we must perhaps conclude that either *Saul* is not a "critical" work (Gide insisted that all his works were critical in content and ironic in nature), or that his theory has exceptions, or that his homosexuality was indeed a defect which he could not overcome (as he is alleged to have confided to a friend in later years). The fact that Gide's works frequently revolve around an "inner stain" (a defect of the personality acquired in childhood), explains his preoccupation with the uncommon and the sickly (as his botanical interest in the unusual species suggests). In *Strait is the Gate* the defect in Alissa's makeup is her fear of becoming like her mother: an unfaithful profligate and the talk of the town. Alissa will use an ascetic morality as a shield against Jérôme and marriage even though her journal reveals that, had Jérôme been more insistent (as Gide was with his wife, Madeleine), she would have married him. Alissa succumbs to her asceticism precisely because Jérôme is not more forceful. On one level Gide is criticising the austerity of the "strait gate," while on another level the indelible spot in Alissa's personality, making her the victim of her asceticism, is the fear of becoming like her mother.

The levels of meaning in *Strait is the Gate* and *The Immoralist* are comparable. Michel's preoccupation with sickness and his inability to tolerate imperfection, when combined with a Nietzschean "readiness" (Gide calls it *disponibilité*) will lead him to sacrifice his wife, Marceline, during his demonic journey from the Alps (where she was recovering from a lung disease) through Italy to North Africa. "Whom will I persuade [says Gide] that this book *[Strait is the Gate]* and *The Immoralist* are twins and that the two subjects grew in my mind concurrently, the excess of one finding a secret permission in the excess of the other, both together forming an equilibrium" (*Journal*, February 7, 1912). This equilibrium was adumbrated in the play

Saul by the Saul-David opposition—Saul's excesses being counteracted by David's. While David's obedience to God should perhaps not be viewed as an excess, in view of Gide's rejection of authoritarian religion he does in fact consider such obedience excessive.

In the biblical version, Saul is rejected by God because he "feared the people, and obeyed their voice" instead of the Lord's (1 Sam. 15:24). The fact that God prefers obedience to sacrificial offerings is echoed in Samuel's reproach to Saul, "to obey *is* better than sacrifice . . . for rebellion *is as* the sin of witchcraft" (1 Sam. 15:23-23). It is useful to note that the action of Gide's play begins with Saul's order to kill the witches; but the witches he wants eliminated are none other than God's minor prophets. What is the meaning of this juxta-position to the biblical text which Gide knew so well and which seems to be the point of departure for his own play? Are we to conclude that Saul, as he himself affirms, not only can no longer pray, but that he is now in direct conflict with God whose power he wants to usurp? "When I alone am capable of knowing the future, I believe I will be able to change it" (p. 16).

In Gide's play we hear Saul saying, "The Philistines came: I was worried: I wanted to do the questioning myself; and since then, God has been silent" (p. 16). Saul's initial disobedience transforms itself into a desire to predict the future. Since it is not possible to know the future, his desire to wrest this power from God, by eliminating the prophet-witches, suggests a wish for equality that goes beyond rebellion. Saul wants to be able to predict the future in order to influence it—he wants to supplant God—thereby adding arrogance to disobedience. It is often said that pride is the greatest of sins, that it always precedes a fall. (It is perhaps not surprising to find Saul surrounded by Lucifer's progeny.) Since the sin of pride consists in man's ambition to fulfill all his potentialities in opposition to God's omniscience, Saul is now doomed to suffer both the consequences of his pride and the agony of his human limitations.

The Bible is consistent in stressing the theme of obedience to God. Ironically, in *The Notebooks of André Walter* and in *Strait is the Gate,* Gide portrays such obedience as leading to the protagonists' premature death. Saul, like Adam and Eve, more independent and more rebellious than Walter or Alissa, has disobeyed God's will. Now that he is an outcast, a fallen man, and since God will not forgive him, Saul, in both the Bible and in Gide's version, has no recourse but to rely on himself. Moreover, Saul is an ambivalent creature whom Gide has created in his own early image; like Gide, he vacillates between his need to love God and his need to explore—having no alternative—the dimensions of his human potential. "I am perfectly willing to love God;—I used to love Him—but He has withdrawn from me—why?" (p. 61). The first devil answers: "To bring us closer together."

The emphasis in Gide's play then shifts from disobedience and self-reliance to profane love. Saul now both loves and hates David. "Everything I find delicious is hostile to me. Delicious! my delicious one! would that I could be with him, a herdsman, beside the streams . . . my soul, which the song stirs ardently, would burn me less—leaping from my lips—toward you—Daoud—my delicious one" (pp. 105-6). Saul later clasps the devils to his breast under the royal tunic as he would no doubt like to clasp David. But as yet David is not only incorruptible, he is God's anointed son. Does he not consult and obey God's word in all matters and concerns? Is he not, in short, God's warrior since Saul is the leader of a thousand men while David is the leader of ten thousand?

The dilemma is such that Saul is too proud to repent and God is seemingly unwilling to forgive without initial repentance. "Bah!" says Saul, "it has been too long now since I have prayed. And even when I did pray, it was the same. The struggle will continue" (p. 86). Saul, now in active opposition to God, at times even seeks David's help. He asks David if he sometimes prays; David answers that he often does. Saul retorts that God never answers prayer, but David wonders, perhaps naively, what a king might ask for that would not be granted.

Saul. And You. What do you ask Him for?
David. Never to become king.
Saul. David! David! Do you want to join forces with me against God?
[p. 104]

To corrupt David, the representative of obedience to God and His imperatives, would be a major victory against God. Saul realizes, however, that this is not possible, and in his anger and frustration he tries to kill David with his spear. But the ambivalence persists, and Saul will alternatively (with Jonathan's intervention) forgive and pursue David. His attempt to kill David intensifies his struggle with God—his wish to silence the authoritarian voice. The impasse is now absolute, because, if Saul loves David, then to kill him would remove the source of temptation, but at the same time it would destroy the object of his love.

Gide's personal impasse and quagmire was to escape the dilemma of his sexual predilections. If Saul, as a character, summarizes the temptations of revolt and eroticism, and if David represents Gide's lingering fidelity to an ascetic Protestant morality, then Saul's death and David's triumph reflect a temporary resolution of the two aspects of Gide's internal conflict. The act of writing *Saul* suggests that the voice of God may still be strong in Gide's ear. The play, therefore, dramatizes the polarization of a moral strife. Saul's death and David's triumph seem to represent the temporary victory of the Authoritarian conscience. The play *Saul* now counterbalances the exuberance of the Humanistic conscience manifest earlier in *Fruits of the Earth* (1897), just as the excesses of *Strait is the Gate* (1909) counterbalance those of *The Immoralist* (1902).

The central theme of the play *Saul* emerges as an attempt on Gide's part to elude himself. If the play is a dramatization of a personal conflict, then Saul's efforts to silence the voice of God, while being in love with his anointed son, David, is the quintessence of Gide's personal drama.

The oscillation between the two poles of Gide's psyche persists, and is recorded artistically, in alternating cycles, for our insights and our delectation, until it is resolved in *The Counterfeiters* (1926): "Does not the extraordinary difficulty I now have in expressing myself also come from the fact that no imaginary characters inhabit me any more and that I strive to speak in my own name only?" (*Journal*, May 2, 1931). Thus *Corydon, If it Die,* and *The Counterfeiters* climax Gide's progression toward self-emancipation from the Authoritarian conscience, i.e., God's internalized voice. Gide's books are the record of this progression: the struggle between the two alternatives providing the necessary tension for his creative genius. When the tension is eliminated, as it was by 1925, the true creative spark dies.

Gide deliberately cultivated this tension on all levels: creative, epistolary, and personal. He recognized how strongly he needed it and how essential it was for his work. Though the duality of his art, for the most part, was spent by the time he published *Oedipus* (1930), it manifested itself on a personal level in his *Journal,* in his relationship with his wife Madeleine, and in his continuing dialogue with his Catholic opponents, particularly with Paul Claudel, Francis Jammes,

Henri Massis, and Charles Du Bos. Gide's trips to Africa and the Soviet Union and his "dialogue" with capitalism *(Voyage to the Congo)* and then with Communism *(Return from the USSR)* suggest that the need for living in a climate of opposing forces had shifted from the artistic to the social level.

Gide's work, for all its diversity and variety, is a search for man's authentic being that lurks behind the façade of convention and the incrustations of stereotype. Gide's early rebellion against authoritarianism and his subsequent "dialogue" with God lead him to supplant God and replace Him with man. Initially, Prometheus steals fire from the gods in order to enlighten man, thus demonstrating that man fulfills himself in opposition to the gods. Ultimately, as Camus phrases it, rebellion transforms itself into affirmation. Affirmation, in turn, leads to authenticity. To reach an authentic state of being, man creates himself anew, each time. But such creativity is not easy when the family, the state, the church, dogma, and society at large stifle man's freedom by imposing ready-made conventions. The past inhibits the free expression of the self. Gide's Oedipus affirms joyfully the fact that he has sprung from the unknown: "No longer any past, no examples to follow, nothing to lean on; I had to create, invent, and discover everything: fatherland, ancestors. . . . No one to pattern myself after, except myself."[3]

This extraordinary self-reliance, this pride, this strength, which is purely human, is brought low only by forces over which man has no control. Birth and death circumscribe man's existence. In between man creates an authentic being only by challenging those forces that inhibit his "growth." Wisdom begins with the revolt of Prometheus, says Gide, with his challenge to the gods, and ends, of necessity, with the deification of man. Prometheus's fire is, ultimately, man's fire and it comes from within. It illumines.

Can man, coming out of the allegorical cave, bear to look at these implications, at this fire's brightness, and carry through with the difficult task that lies ahead? Can existential man, who no longer believes in a Platonic ideal, create his own essence and walk on his own two feet unaided by God? Gide believes that man can and must. Gide's life and his work demonstrate that man should, whenever possible, steal God's fire and use it wisely. This "dreadful freedom," as Sartre calls it, is humanity's greatest challenge. Will man create or destroy? Man, alone, responsible only to and for Himself, can, if He so wills it, build a New Jerusalem. Oedipus's answer to the Sphinx's riddle was and always inevitably will be Man.

II

Hemingway's
Battle with God

Time may show it *[The Old Man and the Sea]* to be the best single
piece of any of us.

William Faulkner

Ernest Hemingway in 1958 at age 59.

INTRODUCTION

The Old Man and the Sea has most frequently been interpreted as a fish story, as a pagan parable, as a Christian parable, and as a parable of the writer and his art. My purpose is to provide a new focus on these interpretations—particularly the pagan and the Christian—and show that the pagan one corresponds to Santiago's consciousness, while the Christian one reflects, not Hemingway's persona, but a collective id manifest in the imagery and symbolism of the Western Christian tradition.

The themes that Hemingway weaves into *The Old Man and the Sea,* like counterpoint in a Bach fugue, explore the ideas of pride in killing and victory in conquest as opposed to humility in defeat and suffering in abnegation. Santiago is a pagan Catholic whose age, pride, honor, and courage force him to prove that pain is nothing to a man and that a fisherman can perform miracles. This Cuban protagonist of Spanish birth harpoons marlin like a matador and suffers pain like a Christ figure. Using Santiago as a symbolic namehead Hemingway fuses the themes into a moving experience of life and death.

The novel's form, perhaps more accurately than the substance itself, is an important aspect of Hemingway's persona, reflecting his own values and beliefs. Thus, three narrative voices—Santiago's conscious experience, the pervasive Christ motif which is outside Santiago's experience, and the novel's poetic form—combine to give us fourth and fifth dimensions which constitute a prose that is harder to write than poetry (says Hemingway) and which, he says, has never before been written. What follows is an interpretation of pride and rebellion as manifest in *The Old Man and the Sea:* Hemingway's battle with God.

PRIDE, *THE OLD MAN AND THE SEA*

i

Readers familiar with Hemingway's life know that he was converted in the 1930s and that in spite of his suicide he died a Roman Catholic. Commentators, however, both here and abroad generally agree that while "technically" a Roman Catholic, Hemingway never really entirely accepted Christianity. E. M. Halliday states that Hemingway's most devout characters, like Anselmo in *For Whom the Bell Tolls* and Santiago in *The Old Man and the Sea* disclaim their religiosity and pray mechanically.[1] Carlos Baker says that Hemingway was a sceptic and generally superstitious in the presence of mysteries. He sees Hemingway's religion as a kind of nonintellectualized humanism which prompted him to turn to and then away from the Church.[2] Whatever Hemingway's personal views, says Joseph Waldmeir, he always had the utmost respect for Christians, provided they lived like Christians. There is no evidence of intentional blasphemy in any of his works.[3] Leo J. Hertzel states that

unlike so-called Catholic writers like Léon Bloy or Bernanos, Hemingway gives his Catholicism no flicker of light from beyond the finite, the human and the temporal. He writes as a naturalist, and there is no supernatural dimension in his fiction. The Catholic Church is treated something like bullfighting is treated—it is presented as a colorful institution with richness, tradition, ritual and discipline, but it provides no convenient miracles. What this amounts to is that Hemingway uses the religion chiefly as a kind of literary ingredient.[4]

Françoise Gaston-Chérau maintains that Catholicism is not an integral part of Hemingway's work even though a number of his characters profess to be Catholics.[5] Claude-Edmonde Magny goes so far as to state that Hemingway's world is an atheistic one.[6] In the same vein, C. N. Stavrou believes that in Hemingway's world human existence moves inexorably toward futility, vacancy, destruction, and waste; that the tug in the direction of death, nothingness, and despair is one of the most significant ingredients in his work.[7] In *The Sun Also Rises* Jake characterizes Roman Catholicism as a "beautiful religion," but when he tries to pray and fails he concedes that prayer is "a futile gesture." In *The Old Man and the Sea* Santiago says a few perfunctory prayers, then goes about the more important and pressing business of catching the marlin and fighting sharks. There is also Hemingway's "memorable and excoriating travesty of the Lord's Prayer" in the short story "A Clean, Well-Lighted Place," in which he anticipates Sartre and the existentialists:

Our nada who art in nada, nada be thy name thy kingdom nada thy will be nada in nada as it is in nada. Give us this nada our daily nada and nada us our nada as we nada our nadas and nada us not into nada but deliver us from nada; pues nada. Hail nothing full of nothing, nothing is with thee.

Hemingway was not a pious man. Proud yes, highly competitive yes, but not particularly religious in the Christian sense. Carlos Baker says that Hemingway "missed the ghostly comforts of institutionalized religion as a man who is cold and wet misses the consolations of good whiskey."[8]

Many readers of *The Old Man and the Sea,* aware of the highly developed Christ motif, keep wondering about its relevance and commenting on its significance. John Killinger, Robert O. Stephens, Carlos Baker, Joseph Waldmeir, Leo Gurko, Clinton S. Burhans, Arvin R. Wells, Philip Young, Richard B. Hovey, among others, explicate the novel in relation to it.[9] If Hemingway's fictional world is not fundamentally Christian, why the heavy use of Christian symbolism? Such saturation has prompted a number of commentators to see the novel as a Christian parable, though, in my opinion, the work should probably be classified as a pagan poem to existential man. Differences in interpretation, while not necessarily exclusive, may stem from the fact that the novel's explicators have not always made a sufficiently clear delineation of the levels on which the story is being read. Nor have the points of view from which it is told and lived been analyzed with the same precision which Santiago uses to catch fish.

The novel is first of all about an old Cuban fisherman who goes out too far on the Gulf Stream, hooks a 1600 pound marlin, fights him for three days, harpoons him on the third, lashes him to his skiff, and sails back to Cuba only to lose the marlin to the sharks during the return trip. This is Santiago's experience on the most elemental and physical level.

Secondly, on the conscious, verbalized, and symbolic levels the interpretations of the novel as parable rely on the fact that Hemingway gives it a prominent Christ motif. It should be noted that this motif has no bearing on Santiago's own evaluation of his experience. Santiago is a proud and not uncomplicated man, but his view of the world does not include the artistic dimension Hemingway structures for the reader. There is a fictional level (perhaps the fifth dimension Hemingway has from time to time alluded to) that carries beyond Santiago's consciousness to include the Christian tradition. Critics have taken for granted the fact that Santiago's suffering is comparable to Christ's. But the reasons for comparing Santiago to Christ, while including obvious allusions to the way both men suffered and were "crucified," have not received sufficiently detailed treatment.

Is the comparison between the two men important because in Hemingway's story "Today is Friday" one of the Roman soldiers admires the stoic way Christ took his suffering and that therefore Santiago's ordeal, like the Crucifixion, is the epitome of grace under stress? Such an answer, while relevant, is perhaps also too facile. Besides, it minimizes the artistry of the novel. The effect of the christological imagery on the reader, contrary to expectations generated by its use, is essentially non-Christian. Since biblical parallelisms between Santiago's experience and Christ's are given such prominence, the reasons for their inclusion must be more than comparative. From an artistic point of view the dominant reason would be to provide information on a religious and cultural heritage. But why should Hemingway want to do that? The answer is already contained in the title of this study.

Critics have emphasized Santiago's heroism, his endurance under pressure, his transfiguration, his love, his humility, his Christlike attributes, his kinship with nature and champions, his pride, his embodiment of the American pioneer spirit, even his ties with society, but no one has analyzed Santiago's challenge to Creation and by extension Hemingway's battle with God.

Santiago's ordeal through the stages of separation, vision, and return mirrors a heroic cycle of trial through endurance which, in spite of Hemingway's carefully structured parallel with Christianity, is more typical of the initiation rites of primitive societies than it is of the Crucifixion. On a cultural level the novel mirrors the cycle by which a moribund tradition must perhaps be slain and resurrected. The novel's Christian symbolism suggests that the tradition Hemingway is slaying is Christianity (the fish). Santiago's vision and message will be resurrected through Manolin (meaning Immanuel or the Messiah). When Santiago returns he ties the rope of his skiff to a rock. In Christian symbolism a ship represents the Church. God founded his Church upon the rock of St. Peter. Appropriately, Pedrico, Manolin's friend, gets the dead marlin's head.

Of what relevance are such details and is the symbolism forced? Answers to these questions will be forthcoming and will depend in part on an explication of the separate as well as overlapping narrative points of view. Who is telling the story and how and why? Hemingway, obviously, but also sometimes Santiago. Hemingway's consciousness, however, is not Santiago's, nor is Hemingway's use of Christian imagery and detail part of Santiago's world. If viewed as extraneous fictional elements, the biblical allusions force an extrinsic reading of the novel. By extrinsic I mean that the reader can bring biblical knowledge and Christian symbolism to his interpretation of the story. There is also the question of artistic consciousness and the reader's willingness to accept poetic ambiguity, resonance, symbolism and linguistic economy as integral parts of the book. Poetry sometimes requires an extrinsic reading of the poem based on the intrinsic (internal) signs provided by the author. Good poetry does not tell, it suggests. It works in images and metaphors from within the poem—linguistic "tricks" which make it possible for the reader to abstract the idea the author wishes to convey. The Christ motif in *The Old Man and the Sea* provides the imagery which the reader follows, but the idea that emerges is non-Christian. Why, for instance, does Pedrico get the marlin's head? Is this detail to be overlooked? What happens if we pursue it?

Pedro, whose diminutive is Pedrico, is the Spanish for Peter. Saint Peter is known as the Great Fisherman and is the patron saint of fishermen. Peter is the leading Apostle of Christ (Acts 1:13, 15, 2:14; 1 Pet. 1:1; 2 Pet. 1:1). Peter's name always *heads* the Twelve (Acts 1:13). Peter declared Christ's messiahship to the Disciples at a time of doubt and confusion (Matt. 16:13-16; Mark 8:27-29; Luke 9:18-20). Peter was frequently the *head* spokesman for the disciples. He took *the lead* in investigating the women's story of the open tomb (John 20:2). Peter was the *leader* of the apostolic church. He was the *first* to open the doors of the church to Gentiles. He participated in the *first* Jerusalem congress. The Roman Catholic church considers Peter as its *first* pope. Peter is the *head* of the Christian church. Finally, Peter, at his own request, was crucified *head* "downward; not otherwise."[10]

Even though Pedrico's role is a minor one, the use of his name is consistent with the novel's Christ motif. Santiago's desire that Manolin give "the head" of the giant fish to Pedrico is given specific emphasis by being repeated twice.[11] Manolin, the new Messiah, gets the marlin's spear (p. 24). This spear is also described as a rapier, which is a straight two-edged sword with a narrow pointed blade. In Christian symbolism the sword denotes spiritual warfare against the forces of evil (Matt. 10:34; Rev. 1:16; 19:21). In Eph. 6:17 "the sword of the Spirit" is "the word of God." Such biblical knowledge is extrinsic to the novel, yet it provides information, only hinted at in the narrative, which is essential for a correct reading of its intent, since Hemingway does not provide (nor would it be desirable to do so) a running commentary of his own. The names Santiago, Manolin, and Pedrico, three very frequent and familiar Spanish names, work well in symbolic association with each other. Hemingway had read his Bible and he was thoroughly familiar with both the Old and the New Testaments.

The reader is therefore perhaps justified in concluding that Santiago is the symbolic Father who teaches his symbolic Son and disciple, Manolin. After Santiago has once again proved his superiority as a fisherman by catching the largest marlin, Manolin, like Christ, will leave his parents in order to follow the teachings of his master, Santiago. "He that loveth father or mother more than me is not worthy of me: and he that loveth son or daughter more than me is not worthy of me. And he that taketh not his cross, and followeth after me, is not worthy of me" (Matt. 10:37–38). Manolin, the Messiah, gets the dead fish's spear which, in Christian terms, is also the sword of faith, and the reader infers that he, together with Pedrico, will spread the "good news" of Santiago's "victory." After his ordeal Santiago falls asleep in a cruciform position on his newspapers (good news?). We have God, His Son, and Saint Peter—a trinity, the beginning of a new faith, the cell of a new religion, the founding rock of a new church. (Every word of the title *The Old Man and the Sea* is composed of three letters.) Hemingway has used the archetypal quest not only as a structural device, but as a metaphor for the cultural quest to revitalize the dead God—that is, the cultural heritage—by resurrecting the Son. A myth is reborn and as though made new for an existential age.

Robin H. Farquhar sees the dénouement of *The Old Man and the Sea* as an ironic epilogue designed to "bring home" the point of the novel.[12] Since the tourists (presumably American) mistake the skeleton of the gigantic marlin for that of a shark it is clear that the secret which Santiago has discovered and its importance have been left at sea with the flesh of the fish. Santiago leaves his "vision" on the Gulf Stream, but Manolin and the reader understand. The sharing of Santiago's achievement is limited to those few, such as Manolin and Pedrico, who are initiated into the rites of this kind of fishing or writing. Manolin will be the new savior and Pedrico the new pope. Armed with the marlin's spear they will fish in Santiago's name and propagate "his message."

To accomplish the revitalization of man that this message requires, the author floats his persona midway between Santiago the proud, aged fisherman and Hemingway the proud, aging writer. An unlucky, routinely religious Santiago goes way out on the eighty-fifth day in order to rescue his pride, his honor, and his courage—his Spanish *pundonor*. Hemingway's narrative voice, sometimes obtrusive, most of the time muted, structures Santiago's ordeal as an epic correlation to the Crucifixion.

A number of commentators have mentioned the relevance of pride to the meaning of the novel, but none has given it central billing nor related it to Hemingway's attempt to substitute a naturalistic religion of man for an entire religious tradition. Astonishing perhaps is the fact that one of Hemingway's favorite themes, the solitude of man, should in this story have jelled into something beyond itself, be the catalyst for ideas affecting all men, and serve as an example and an ideal for man vis-à-vis himself and the world. While Hemingway never seems to have thought much of Christ's injunction to turn the other cheek, or of the Sermon on the Mount, the ordeal on the cross seems to have impressed him considerably. Repeatedly, Santiago's experience and physical suffering are compared to Christ's agony, yet Hemingway's message is one of pride rather than humility—an exaltation of man with only perfunctory obeisance to God.

After the critical debacle of *Across the River and into the Trees,* Hemingway the famous writer, mythmaker, fisherman, and killer of lions was out for big literary game—something to reaffirm him once again as a master craftsman. Santiago, the unlucky fisherman, like Hemingway the writer, wants to redeem his tarnished reputation— restore his injured pride. To do so, Santiago will go out too far in his quest and catch the largest marlin ever seen, while Hemingway will not only write a brilliant novel, but resurrect a Messiah who will embody and perpetuate Santiago's message of undefeat. This is "big game" and the measure of Hemingway's success must be determined in part by the fact that his Nobel Prize citation referred specifically to his achievement in *The Old Man and the Sea.**

award

ii

Santiago, the old man of the sea, is a thin, gaunt, wrinkled, and widowed Cuban fisherman who has been fishing the Gulf Stream without a catch for eighty-four consecutive days. The sail of his skiff, like the shirt on his back, whose patches have been faded to many different shades by the sun, looks like "the flag of permanent defeat." Handling heavy fish on the cords has left deep-creased scars on his hands that are as "old as erosions in a fishless desert" (p. 10).

After the first *forty* fishless days Santiago's young helper Manolin, who used to fish with him, was ordered by his parents to go in another

---

*The Old Man and the Sea was first published by *Life* magazine on September 1, 1952, then on September 8 in book form by Scribner's. Hemingway's Pulitzer Prize for the novel was announced on May 4, 1953 and the Nobel Prize on October 28, 1954. The Cuban government awarded him the order of Carlos Manuel de Cespedes, the highest honor it could bestow on a foreigner on July 21, 1954, his fifty-fifth birthday.

boat because the old man was *salao*—"the worst form of unlucky" (p. 9). Santiago is suffering from bad luck, loneliness, old age, and "permanent defeat." With forty as some kind of magical, mysterious, and influential number, Manolin's parents order him to fish in another boat since God seems to have withdrawn His favors from Santiago's skiff.

The biblical resonance of "forty days" and "fishless desert," two early instances of the novel's highly developed Christ motif, leads the reader, subliminally, to associate events in Santiago's recent past with Christ's sojourn in the wilderness (Mark 1:13) and Moses' forty days on Mount Sinai (Exod. 24:18, 34:28). Numbers (14:33) records Israel's wilderness wandering as covering forty years.

Santiago is the victim not only of divine disfavor, but also of social ridicule and pity. Younger fishermen make fun of him while the older ones "speak politely" in his presence of the current and the depths at which they drift their lines (p. 11). With his bad luck and no fish to sell and no money Santiago must accept food from Martin, the owner of the Terrace. But it is the boy, Manolin, who takes care of him. Since the residents of the village have lost faith in the old man's ability to catch fish they see him perhaps in his final decline. Only Manolin has not lost faith: "'I know you did not leave me because you doubted' [says the old man]. 'It was papa made me leave. I am a boy and I must obey him.' 'I know,' the old man said. 'It is quite normal.' 'He hasn't much faith.' 'No,' the old man said. 'But we have. Haven't we?'" (pp. 10–11).

In spite of his age, Santiago's shoulders and neck are still powerful and strong. His eyes have remained cheerful, confident, and un-defeated. His vision is good—better than the vision of younger fishermen who have not gone turtling. If eyes are the mirror of the soul, and the Gulf Stream Hemingway once described in *Green Hills of Africa* is the flow of life itself,* then we too should keep faith with

---

*"when, on the sea, you ... know that this Gulf Stream you are living with, knowing, learning about, and loving, has moved, as it moves, since before man, and that it has gone by the shoreline of that long, beautiful, unhappy island since before Columbus sighted it and that the things you find out about it, and those that have always lived in it are permanent and of value because that stream will flow, as it has flowed, after the Indians, after the Spaniards, after the British, after the Americans and after all the Cubans and all the systems of governments, the richness, the poverty, the martyrdom, the sacrifice and the venality and the cruelty are all gone as the high-piled scow of garbage, bright-colored, white-flecked,

this "strange old man" whose eyes are the deep blue color of the Stream, who could once, like a cat or a lion, see in the dark, and who now lives in a shack made with fronds from the royal palm.

While eyes are important in themselves, thematically (much is made of the marlin's eye, shark eyes, cat eyes, a "glimpse of vision"[p. 94], etc.) they serve to highlight the discrepancy between what the villagers see and what Santiago is—between appearance and reality, between what Santiago can still do and what others think he can, between past achievements and present failure. Santiago may seem to be on his last legs, but there is an inner, invisible strength of heroic proportions that will lead him to prove once more that he is still The Champion—*El Campeón*. Thus, one of the themes of *The Old Man and the Sea*, as it was the subject of "The Undefeated," is the gap between outward failure and inner pride, thereby suggesting that point of view is a relevant if not important issue.

Charles K. Hofling, M.D., is of the opinion that the lessening of Santiago's strength due to old age, his loneliness, his ill fortune, his diminished reputation, and his increasing dependence upon the boy, Manolin, are the source of a depression which has affected his self-esteem. Since he was "born to be a fisherman," his sense of identity, his sense of purpose, and his sense of worthwhileness are entirely bound up in his occupational role. Santiago's depression, says Hofling, is the result of shame and narcissistic injury.[13] We might expect other men, less proud than Santiago, to accept the decline that comes with age— to accept the natural and inevitable rhythm of life and death. Santiago apparently will not.

While profoundly attuned to nature's rhythms Santiago is also in

---

ill-smelling, now tilted on its side, spills off its load into the blue water, turning it a pale green to a depth of four or five fathoms as the load spreads across the surface, the sinkable part going down and the flotsam of palm fronds, corks, bottles, and used electric light globes, seasoned with an occasional condom or a deep floating corset, the torn leaves of a student's exercise book, a well-inflated dog, the occasional rat, the no-longer-distinguished cat; all this well shepherded by the boats of the garbage pickers who pluck their prizes with long poles, as interested, as intelligent, and as accurate as historians; they have the viewpoint; the stream, with no visible flow, takes five loads of this a day when things are going well in La Habana and in ten miles along the coast it is as clear and blue and unimpressed as it was ever before the tug hauled out the scow; and the palm fronds of our victories, the worn light bulbs of our discoveries and the empty condoms of our great loves float with no significance against one single, lasting thing—the stream." (New York: Charles Scribner's Sons, 1935), pp. 149-50.

rebellion against nature. The fish and the stars are his brothers and while he says he "must kill" (p. 75) the fish, he is glad he does "not have to try to kill the stars," or the moon, or the sun (p. 75). These are strange thoughts for an old man, thoughts which would seem to imply that if stars were as accessible as fish man would have to try to kill them too. Whatever for? The answer to this question challenges all notions that Santiago is a Christ figure because it implies such extraordinary faith in man's ability to conquer, in man's supremacy, in man's power, in his intelligence, and in his need to assert this manliness. Man takes pleasure in giving death, says Hemingway, because in this way he can usurp one of the godlike attributes.[14] The very need to assimilate such strength and dominion implies pride and pride in turn can lead to rebellion either against nature, or against God, or both. Santiago, for the sake of his pride, is rebelling against old age and death, but Hemingway, through the novel's persona, seems to be challenging the Deity.

Santiago's *pundonor* (a Spanish word meaning honor, probity, courage, self-respect, and pride) makes him "go out too far," kill a marlin, question the notion of "sin," fight "evil" sharks, and return half-dead yet somehow triumphant. Santiago is not just fishing for food. The Christ motif and symbolism are too pronounced, in fact so pronounced that commentators have alluded to the Eucharist, the Crucifixion, and in some cases to a fish-Christ identity. The best commentaries have separated the novel's Christ motif from its pagan message, but for many commentators the christological imagery has tended to obscure its anti-Christian emphasis. This is not to say that Santiago's ordeal and Christ's are not comparable. Hemingway makes it clear that they are. " 'Ay,' he [Santiago] said aloud. There is no translation for this word and perhaps it is just a noise such as a man might make, involuntarily, feeling the nail go through his hands and into the wood" (p. 107).

Many other Santiago-Christ associations occur, as, for instance, in the description of the old man's return trip up the hill to his hut. Santiago is carrying the skiff's mast on his back and falls under its weight as Christ fell under the weight of the cross on his way to Calvary. Santiago goes to sleep with his arms outstretched in a cruciform position. Even though he is not yet dead, there are many additional allusions to and symbolic analogies with the Crucifixion. John Halverson mentions the fact that Manolin will bring Santiago a clean shirt, as Joseph of Arimathaea brought clean linen to wrap the body of Christ. Manolin will also bring "stuff from the drugstore" for Santiago's mutilated hands as ointments were brought for the dead Christ. The boy stands watch over the sleeping fisherman as a watch was set over the sepulchre of Christ.[15]

While critics have elucidated the many different aspects of the Christ motif, they differ in their interpretation as well as in their evaluation of it. Halverson concludes from his study that Santiago's ordeal and unconscious example are "profoundly Christian, indeed an *imitatio Christi*."[16] Clinton Burhans says that the meaning of the old man's experience "is the humility and love of Christ and the interdependence which they imply."[17] Richard B. Hovey, however, thinks the Christ imagery is only tentative and not exclusively Christian.[18] Carlos Baker says that Santiago's triumph in defeat is not necessarily a Christian victory, though Baker sees Santiago's love of the fish and the experience itself as profoundly Christian. Melvin Backman says that Santiago is a crucified matador—that his ordeal and triumph, defeat and victory are both Christian and pagan. Nemi d'Agostino, on the contrary, affirms that the novel's religious or mystical implications are forced and its symbolism a fictitious disguise. In the same vein Arvin R. Wells believes that while Hemingway uses Christian symbols, the thrust of the story is primarily pagan. Philip Young says that *The Old Man and the Sea* is a natural parable in the form of a metaphor whose message is that the world not only breaks but crucifies. Joseph Waldmeir feels that Hemingway has elevated his philosophy of Manhood to the level of a religion. Leo Gurko states that the connections with Jesus, half-man, half-God, draw Santiago out of a purely human frame of reference toward the superhuman.[19] Robert O. Stephens says that Santiago, like Adam, dooms himself to physical deterioration in order to open the way to spiritual enlightenment, i.e., triumph in defeat through stoic virtues of endurance. This, says Stephens, is the moral crest of Hemingway's metaphorical iceberg.*

---

*Santiago exploits his moral nature and rises above his animal state, says Stephens, by usurping a godlike attribute: knowledge. The moral discovery of *The Old Man and the Sea* is that man escapes from the trap of death (biology) by rising above death through achievement. "Hemingway's Old Man and the Iceberg," pp. 295–304.

We see, therefore, that many commentators favor a non-Christian view. While they generally agree that the Christ motif adds depth to the story, their interpretation as well as their evaluation of it differ. Carlos Baker for instance feels that Santiago has essential qualities like gallantry and militance which clearly associate him with the character and personality of Christ in the Gospel stories.[20] But I see little to distinguish Santiago's gallantry, militance, and endurance (Baker's words) from similar qualities portrayed by brave men everywhere. More specifically, where is the Sermon on the Mount, the Golden Rule, the need to walk the second mile, or turn the other cheek? While Baker is right in stressing Santiago's humility, it is a humility of strength. The Christ motif is Hemingway's, not Santiago's (Santiago is blissfully oblivious of it all) and it is essential that we keep this dual point of view in mind. In fact, Hemingway sets Santiago up as a kind of superman rivaling the Deity. Santiago may be killing fish, but Hemingway is killing God.* This is why Santiago is not tempted to cut the line and let the big fish go, as Norman Mailer says he should have been, because the despair and pride which drove him too far out in the first place also prompt him to hang on. He would rather die than lose the fish.[21] "You are killing me, fish," says Santiago, but "I do not care who kills who" (p. 92).

John Killinger, in his fine existential study of Hemingway, says that "when God is overthrown and the world is without values, then the rebel must set up his own laws and moral codes."[22] Santiago, from his boyhood onward, has always been self-reliant. He knows the ocean, he knows the weather, and he fishes with precision. The laws and moral code that he observes, except for the perfunctory and ritual use of prayer, are his own and those of the sea. The marlin will teach him dignity, nobility, and endurance, but the law of the sea, and this is the essential point, is survival.† Furthermore, Hemingway's precise

---

*In *Ernest Hemingway: A Life Story,* Carlos Baker refers to a statement Hemingway once made about the content of his fiction and the hidden dynamite within. I interpret some of Hemingway's writings as a timebomb. When the explosion takes place within the reader's mind, it shatters the surface calm, reorders values, and restructures events.

†In *Ernest Hemingway: A Life Story,* p. vii, Carlos Baker says that "the small boy who shouted 'Fraid o'nothing' became the man who discovered that there was plenty to fear, including that vast cosmic nothingness which Goya named

naturalistic descriptions of life in and on the Gulf Stream give us more than local color. Man-of-war birds, as well as dolphin, eat the flying fish, turtles eat the men-of-war, while sharks eat the flippers of the sleeping turtles. Seahawks eat the little birds and so on and so forth. Santiago, as yet another manifestation of natural forces (and the survival in this case is of the most intelligent), catches and destroys a great sixteen-hundred pound marlin.

The laws of nature are a code in themselves, and man, like the marlin which swims for three days against the Gulf Stream, can, as long as he is alive, resist death and affirm his dignity by "swimming" against the current. There is no point in elaborating Hemingway's "code hero" motif since much has already been written on it, but there is great symbolic value for Hemingway and existentialists alike in "swimming against the current." Santiago, like Sisyphus rolling his stone up the mountain, must affirm his identity as a fisherman (since that is what he was "born for") by fishing and proving it up to the very end. "The thousand times that he had proved it meant nothing. Now he was proving it again. Each time was a new time and he never thought about the past when he was doing it" (p. 66).

Men like Santiago, if they believe in themselves, must forever act in order to affirm their selfhood. Jack J. Benson sees the Hemingway protagonist as typically alone, reduced to his selfhood as a kind of place or possession, and struggling against the erosion of time and change. "A threat to selfhood is the ultimate threat, involving the ultimate horror that the irrational forces of the world can accomplish."[23] Men who feel this threat, and the ultimate threat is death, carry the painful responsibility of constantly proving themselves. Santiago's moral code requires that he, as a fisherman, catch fish. Each time "is a new time," regardless of age.

The marlin also has a code which is not without meaning for the

---

Nada. The adolescent, wounded in Italy, learned that no man was exempt from mortality. The romantic activist, the center and in many ways the originator of his own universe, became the pragmatic moralist whose leading aim was to find out how to live life, how to last and (having lasted) how to convert a carefully cultivated stoical fortitude into the stuff of which his fictional heroes were made. The ethical hedonist sought and found a million pleasures while learning, over and over, that human life, his own included, is forever punctuated with pain. *Il faut (d'abord) durer* became his watchword as well as the rule by which he lived until the concept of lasting gave way to an overriding conviction that it was time for him to die."

reader. The hook in the marlin's mouth is perhaps a death metaphor. Since every man is "hooked" from the moment he is born, *is it* not *how* he swims against the "current" that defines his existence and gives meaning to life? The "hook" that leads men and fish to swim against the Stream is an anguish that must be endured, until "the dark water of the true gulf" (not capitalized by Hemingway) which "is the greatest healer that there is" (p. 99) engulfs us all. You fight to survive as the marlin fights and as Santiago fights. This is their code. Like the marlin, Santiago will fight until exhaustion and death lest he fail in his honor, lest he fail the abiding laws of nature.

Existentialists like Heidegger and Sartre view death—one's own as well as God's—as the essential clue to authentic living. It is this one "capital" possibility, always in view from the outset, from which all other possibilities derive their status of radical contingency. What dread, or despair, or alienation reveal to every man is that he is cast into the world in order to die there. To live with death as the supreme and normative possibility of existence is not to reject the world or to refuse participation in its daily preoccupations. On the contrary, it is a refusal to be deceived. To accept death is to heighten the capacity for living which in turn leads to a heightened sense of authentic personal existence.

This sense of existence leads to an exalted sense of the present with its compelling emphasis on being now. Carlos Baker says that the phrase "our one and only life" runs through Hemingway's correspondence with Charles T. Lanham "like a themesong."[24] E. M. Halliday says that Hemingway's suspicion of ultimate doom increases his passionate fondness for being alive. "Extinction may well be the end of all, as the writer of Ecclesiastes repeatedly remarked, but for Hemingway and his heroes this merely emphasizes the need to live each moment properly and skilfully, to sense judiciously the texture of every fleeting act and perception."[25] "Maybe if you found out how to live in it you learned from that what it was all about," says Jake Barnes in *The Sun Also Rises.* Santiago, like Jake, his namesake, has learned what it is all about and goes out once more to prove that he is a man. It is our "performance en route" that counts for good or bad, says Hemingway.[26]

Santiago performs exceptionally well and all the way under constant pressure. This is his (man's) saving grace, his refusal to give up, his fight to the end. Bernard S. Oldsey sees *The Old Man and the Sea* as a return to the theme of the "undefeated," to the winner takes nothing, the man to whom things happen, the man whom the sharks of the world leave with *nada*. [27] This is what it means to be a man cast adrift in a contingent universe, for who can be more alone than Santiago on the Gulf Stream with no relatives and nothing to return to but his shack in the village? Yet Santiago, the tenacious, precise, and intelligent fisherman shows what a man can endure, how he can behave, and how he can affirm his identity in the jaws of sharks, adversity, old age, and even death. Carlos Baker states somewhere that Hemingway considered the *Dignity of Man* as a provisional title for *The Old Man and the Sea*. John Killinger sees in Santiago, who "took his suffering as it came," an almost classical symbol of the dignity of humanism. [28] "I will show them," says Santiago, "what a man can do and what a man endures" (p. 66). Santiago will endure extraordinary privation and suffering to prove that man, of all the beasts, even the lions and the marlins, has the greatest pride and dignity—that man is King.

Santiago's message is that "man can be destroyed but not defeated" (p. 103). Santiago will die, but the example of his heroic struggle will live. To fight heroically is to affirm man's dignity. Stanley Cooperman sees this will to conquer as an echo of the divine but, if I interpret him correctly, only in the sense that Divinity and man's Supreme Will are one and the same. If this is true, then the story of Santiago is a re-emphasis and intensification of one of Hemingway's favorite themes: isolation. The individual confronts his own destiny and redeems it by means of a ritual of manhood. [29]

This is not to say that Santiago does not partake of a certain social ethic. Manolin takes care of him and feeds him and the old man is grateful, although, in his fierce pride, he is obviously also resentful, since he plays a game of make-believe with Manolin that will save face and leave his pride intact. Santiago pretends he has yellow rice and fish when he has none; he pretends he has washed his hands for supper when in fact he has not. This is more than "informed illusion" as one commentator has called it. Santiago must eat, but he must also protect his ego, and "pretense" is the best he can come up with. So his decision to go way out on the eighty-fifth day is a gamble that must pay off. The old man's injured pride can endure no more and he has to take that final chance. William J. Handy says that Santiago's decision to go far out is no more than a conscious attempt to oppose the forces of ill luck and the inevitable demands of a materialistic society. [30] This is true, but if the argument about selfhood and pride holds, then Santiago's venture is also a challenge to man's limitations as well as to the forces of destiny. He is challenging death itself and by extension the Creator who administers it. Or rather, it is Hemingway who challenges the Creator since it is he who uses Christian symbols and it is he who has Santiago slay the fish.

Santiago kills a marlin, but if the Christ motif is more than comparative, Hemingway is out for bigger game than fish. Santiago is unaware of the author's symbols even though Santiago's attitudes and the author's point of view tend to overlap. Santiago embodies all the virtues of a naturalistic humanism whereas Hemingway is replacing Christianity with *pundonor*. While Christ had love and compassion for the poor and the sinful and the meek and the downtrodden, Santiago's love for the fish is primarily the respect one develops for the strength and ability of a worthy opponent. He also feels a love and kinship for all living things including *la mar,* which is what people call the sea in Spanish when they love her (p. 29). But if Santiago's pride is "forced out through the openings in the sieve of his suffering," it is because he has met an opponent who is every bit his equal. In spite of the marlin's size, Santiago wins, and by the time he returns to port his damaged pride has been restored. Does he not dream once more of lions? Has he not challenged the stars, fought sharks, faced death, and brought back a prize? The marlin's skeleton is the incontrovertible evidence. Few recognize it, least of all the tourists. As Santiago struggles up the hill to his shack carrying the mast of his "crucifixion" and collapses on the newspapers with his arms outstretched we sense that his age and the ordeal have at last destroyed him physically, but not spiritually.

Santiago kills fish, in part because he is a fisherman, but also because such acts tend to deny his mortal condition. This is metaphysical revolt, not Christian humility, because it questions the ultimate ends of Creation and protests conditions of mortality imposed on man. The rebel acknowledges yet challenges the power that forces him to live in that condition. Although he defies Creation, Santiago cannot deny it. He cannot suppress Creation, but he can challenge it. He must have the experience of Dominion which can only come through killing. He must continue killing sharks, up to the end, even though he knows it is hopeless, because only in this way can he redeem the initial act of going out "too far" or of "ruining" the marlin or himself. Such desperate heroism is of tragic proportions and relates the old man to Ahab in a way which some commentators have sensed and others denied. Santiago's quest, like Ahab's, is animated by a desire to conquer. Albert Camus says that such an uprising against man's condition "is organized into an over zealous expedition against heaven with the intent of bringing back a prisoner-king whose fall will be proclaimed first, and his death sentence next."[31] "Then when he had seen the fish come out of the water and hang motionless in the sky before he fell, he was sure there was some great *strangeness* [my emphasis] and he could not believe it" (p. 98).

Hemingway refers to the "strange old man" (pp. 14, 66) with the "strange shoulders" (p. 18) who is after a "strange fish" (pp. 48, 67). Santiago finds it "strange" that the fish should have jumped suddenly in the night (p. 84) and he thinks the mako shark has "strange eyes" (p. 101). "Don't you think it is a strange damn story that it should affect all of us (me especially) the way it does?" wrote Hemingway to one of *Life's* editors.[32] In describing a bullfight Hemingway refers to the "strange feeling" of having an animal come toward you consciously seeking to kill you. The bravery of the bullfighter and the beauty of executing the bull are described as "very strange."[33] Have not Freud and the word-picture tests and ideograms of psychology and psychiatry taught us to look for hidden meaning in language?

If we pursue the word "strange" we find that it is associated in Hemingway's lexicon with bullfighting, with death, with beauty, with religious ecstasy, and with immortality:

Now the essence of the greatest emotional appeal of bullfighting is the feeling of immortality that the bullfighter feels in the middle of a great faena . . . He is performing a work of art and he is playing with death.[34]

[Hemingway also writes] the faena that takes a man out of himself and makes him feel immortal while it is proceeding . . . gives him an ecstasy, that is, while momentary, as profound as any religious ecstasy.[35]

The *pundonor* that prompts bullfighters to challenge death is also at the heart of Santiago's pride. This is a theme Melvin Backman has emphasized in an excellent article entitled "Hemingway: The Matador and the Crucified."[36] Santiago shares with the matadors "the feeling of rebellion against death which comes from its administering." A truly great killer, says Hemingway of bullfighters, must love to kill. The best ones have the most highly developed sense of honor and of glory.[37] The way Santiago harpoons the marlin demonstrates that he, like any of the celebrated matadors, is a great killer. Hemingway himself was driven by pride and often discoursed on his favorite subjects of bravery and cowardice. He thought of men without inner dignity as an embarrassment.[38] It is not surprising then that he should have created an old man like Santiago whose actions typify and illustrate the values Hemingway holds dear. "You did not kill the fish only to keep alive and to sell for food, he thought. You killed him for pride and because you are a fisherman" (p. 105).

While Backman and others have demonstrated the similarities between the death of bulls and the way Santiago kills the marlin, no connection has been made between Santiago, the word "strange," and the idea of immortality contained in the above quotations. Yet Santiago's "glimpse of vision" (p. 94) is intended to convey feelings analogous to religious ecstasy. The ritual of administering death gives bullfighters and Santiago a feeling of transcendence verging on immortality. Santiago is faint from the three-day effort, to be sure, but there is another kind of faintness that comes from exposure to what is "strange"—to the mystery of things. "Then the fish came alive, with his death in him, and rose high out of the water showing all his great length and width and all his power and his beauty" (p. 94).

Santiago thinks he feels the fish's heart as he pushes on the harpoon shaft (p. 95). He is now at the quick of things and the revelation is death. Death is at the heart of life. This is the meaning of the "strange" experience and of his "vision"—inevitable, irreconcilable, and irrevocable death. Death is what gives meaning to life. This, as we have seen, is the theme the existentialists have been stressing and which John Killinger in *Hemingway and the Dead Gods* has written persuasively about. But Killinger's analysis of *The Old Man and the Sea* is very short, so it is perhaps appropriate to elaborate the point since Hemingway seems, as he did in *Green Hills of Africa,* to be looking for the connection between hunting animals (or fish) as a sportsman while hunting values against animal death as a writer.

One need not be an existentialist, however, to find the subject of death in Hemingway's writings. Commentators as diverse as William B. Dillingham, Ivan Kashkeen, G.-A. Astre, Quentin Ritzen,[39] and Granville Hicks believe that the bedrock subject of practically everything

Hemingway wrote was man's confrontation with death.* Hemingway himself has revealed the nature of this constant and pervasive theme. "The only place where you could see life and death, i.e., violent death now that the wars were over, was in the bull ring . . . and one of the simplest things of all and the most fundamental is violent death."[40] Hemingway insisted that the bullfights were not cruel spectacles invented for the satisfaction of man's primitive blood lust. Dillingham, in a perceptive essay, says they are "symbolic dramas of man's *ideal* confrontation of death." The bull ring, says Dillingham, is an inspiring metaphor for anyone seeking the talisman of meaningful personal conduct in the face of inevitable destruction. "Hemingway understood the ritual value of the ceremony and sensed that its ultimate aim was to objectify the dignity of man facing death. He understood that the courage and skill and restraint of the matador represented a way of life through which man might—if not defeat death as he does the bull—at least meet it on his own terms."[41]

Meeting death on his own terms is in part the reason behind Santiago's decision to venture out so far. If this is so, it is difficult to agree with Jackson J. Benson that little heroic energy radiates outward from Santiago's epic encounter.[42] Too proud to be the laughing stock of the village or to accept his physical decline, Santiago will challenge nature and die, if necessary, rather than live rejected and humiliated by God, nature, and his fellow fishermen. Such feelings explain why he is never tempted to let go of the line, not even for one moment. In his play *The Flies* Sartre says that "life begins on the far-side of despair." It is perhaps such despair that has driven Santiago to challenge death since he can no longer live without honor. His pride, like the lions, is all he has left. Better to die than to live with the indifferent, mocking, and pitying glances of the villagers. If, as Sartre's play *No Exit* suggests, one's sense of identity is mirrored in the eyes

---

*Granville Hicks writes: "It would be difficult to find an author who has written of death as often and as consistently as has Hemingway. At one time or another he has described the death of ants, salamanders, grasshoppers, and fish: how hyenas die, how to kill kudu, the proper way to execute horses, how bulls are slain, how soldiers die, death in childbirth and death by suicide, death alone and death in group: selfish death, sacrificing death and graceful death." As quoted by Killinger, p. 17. Carlos Baker in *Ernest Hemingway: A Life Story*, p. 77, writes that in 1921 Hemingway wished the family a Merry Christmas, but not a Happy New Year, "Any new year, said he, morosely, was just one more lurch nearer the grave."

of the beholder, then eighty-four luckless days are too much for the proud fisherman to bear. Santiago sees *salao* reflected on the faces of those who look at him. To improve his luck he decides to gamble with eighty-five and asks Manolin to buy a lottery ticket for him with that number on it. He will then gamble with his life and emerge a "winner" with "nothing."

But in order to prove his worth Santiago overextends himself and "breaks something" in his chest. Death, as Bickford Sylvester sums up the situation, "is the final concomitant of life in a champion's combat with nature."[43] But death is every living thing's final concomitant, not alone the champion's. Hemingway's death roster includes people, bulls, big game, birds, fish, and ants. When Katherine Barkley and Robert Jordan die, it is tragic. But Hemingway also handles death with an ironic and even comic touch. In *Green Hills of Africa* bird and hyena shooting become a joke—a type of black humor. If Hemingway killed, the joke was on the birds and M'Cola, his African gun bearer, would shake his head and laugh. If Hemingway missed, he was the clown of the piece and M'Cola would look at him and shake with laughing. "Only the hyenas were funnier," says Hemingway.*

The "classic hyena," the hyena that feeds on carrion, the hyena that skulks in the night eating the bones of dead animals bears the brunt of Hemingway's symbolic, grotesque, yet humorous attack on death itself. Is there anything funnier, he seems to say, than death feeding on itself? Shooting animals is to consciously experience the acceleration of death. To kill an animal is to momentarily and vicariously become God—He who gives life and who takes it away. That is why, whenever Hemingway misses, the joke is on him, for he has claimed a power which he has not been able to deliver. His superior role has reversed itself and now the joke is on the would-be killer. He has tried to play God but his incompetence has transformed him into

---

*"It was funny to M'Cola to see a hyena shot . . . There was that comic slap of the bullet and the hyena's agitated surprise to find death inside of him . . . to see that electric speed that meant that he was racing the little nickelled death inside him. But the great joke of all, the thing M'Cola waved his hands across his face about, and turned away and shook his head and laughed, ashamed even of the hyena; the pinnacle of hyenic humor, was the hyena, the classic hyena, that hit too far back while running, would circle madly, snapping and tearing at himself until he pulled his own intestines out, and then stood there, jerking them out and eating them with relish " (pp. 37–38.)

a clown. The same reasoning transforms the hyena into a superclown since we have a death scavenger in its death-throes devouring its own entrails.

In *Death in the Afternoon* Hemingway pushes this sense of humor farther than we might want to follow by describing the tragedy and inherent comedy of a picador's horse gored by a bull—the grotesque humor of a once noble horse now reduced to skin and bones and the ignominious spectacle of his defeat, of helpless spindly legs and trailing entrails.

While animal death can have its comic asides, there is no humor in *The Old Man and the Sea*. This may be due to Santiago's play for the highest stakes—honor in life—but also to Hemingway's apparent desire to replace Christianity with his own brand of stoic humanism. In this novel, as in so much of Hemingway's work, the moment of death and the act of killing are central. Santiago believes that in spite of the brotherhood of all things killing is necessary and inevitable. The fish is his brother but he "must kill him and keep strong to do it" (p. 59). Unlike Lautréamont Hemingway does not make fun of the Deity. In *The Songs of Maldoror*, Lautréamont both apes and mocks the Creator, but Hemingway is perhaps too serious about his own intent or the heroic aspect of Christ to spoof him.

"Christ, I did not know he was so big."
"I'll kill him though," he said. "In all his greatness and his glory."
[p. 66]

"Christ," "greatness," and "glory" remind us of "the Kingdom and the power, and the glory" of the Lord's Prayer. The Christian and pagan themes of the novel blend here and overlap. "Christ" is Santiago's exclamation, on the one hand, but also, on the other, in association with "greatness" and "glory," Hemingway's equation of fish with Deity. The word "Christ" is an interjection but also a word of identification. It functions as a pun thereby giving two simultaneous ideas. The simultaneity of narrative meaning and points of view are further reinforced by the context. We have here two types of William Empson's "ambiguity." Ambiguity is not carelessness but intentional and due to the richness of poetic speech and verbal nuance, it thus elicits alternative reactions to the same piece of language.[44]

In primitive and mediaeval Christian art the fish was a symbol of Christ. The origin is to be found in the initial letters of the names and titles of Jesus in Greek: Jesus Christ, Son of God, Saviour, which spell the Greek word for "fish":$\iota \chi o \nu \varsigma$. The symbol of the fish in catacombs served to transmit a secret message. Does not the marlin's capture and death transmit a secret and symbolic message of its own? If the fish's demise represents the death of God, then there is a critical transference of identity from fish to Santiago—from the dead to the living. When the mako takes forty pounds from the marlin's side (remember the biblical resonance of forty) Santiago feels as though he himself has been hit. As he sails back to port with the fish lashed to the skiff Santiago wonders: "Is he bringing me in or am I bringing him in?" (p. 99). They sail together "like brothers" now that Santiago's faith in himself has been reconfirmed. When he returns to port his example inspires his disciple Manolin.

We have mentioned the Messianic aspect of the name Manolin—the diminutive for the Spanish Manuel which in English is Immanuel; "the true *God with us,* the Saviour, the Christ." Immanuel means "God is with" and that his message is true.[45] Sheridan W. Baker observes that Manolin is Santiago's disciple of strength and hope, since Manuel is the name not only of the Messiah, but also of the bullfighter in "The Undefeated."[46] Words like "serve," and "faith," allusions to charity and hope, and Santiago's "last supper" with Manolin reinforce the Christ motif and the symbolic dimension of the characters' names. All this takes place on the intrinsic and extrinsic levels, each one reinforcing the other.

The ambiguity of the Christ motif is everywhere. Santiago carries the fish in his right hand. The traitorous left hand is like a claw. Two robbers were crucified with Christ, a traitorous one on the left and a faithful one on the right. Santiago, like Christ, settles against the wood and takes "his suffering as it came" (p. 64). When the fish is killed it hangs momentarily motionless in the air above Santiago, a harpoon in its side. A Roman soldier pierced Christ's side as He too hung motionless in the air.

The same ambiguity that applies to killing the fish also applies to eating it, which has prompted a number of commentators to associate Santiago's eating of the marlin with the Eucharist—that symbolic communion with the flesh and spirit of Christ. While reflecting on the fact that everything kills everything else, Santiago nevertheless concludes that the boy, Manolin, keeps him alive. It is precisely at this moment that Santiago leans over the side of the skiff, pulls loose a piece of meat from the big fish and eats it, noting that it is good, and firm, and juicy. This is Santiago's "communion" with Manolin, not on a transcendent, but on a humanistic level. The act of killing the Christ-fish and of assimilating its flesh serves to reinforce the naturalistic anti-Christian theme of the novel. The marlin represents the best in terms of nobility, dignity, and stoicism that nature can teach. But Santiago goes beyond solitary immersion in nature to think of Manolin and what the boy means to him. The old man and the boy are the focus for much if not everything that is human: friendship, the sharing of food and values, care, help, faith in one another, teaching and learning, respect. To eat the marlin while thinking of Manolin is to commune with all these things, to partake of the human, to strengthen the bonds between men and the values they hold dear. In this context it is appropriate that Clinton S. Burhans, Jr., should develop the theme of Santiago's need for and vision of human solidarity beyond his heroic individualism and tragic absurdity.[47]

Still, if we push the novel's inner logic far enough we are left not so much with love and communion, which as themes seem to me secondary, but with Santiago's example of pride, courage, and stoic endurance. Along with Hemingway's message that "living death" is at the heart of things emerges a composite picture of human dignity based on a full appreciation of life and what a man can do. This message of ethical fortitude is based on the laws of survival in nature but also on human laws of cooperation and inspiration. In this context it is difficult to agree with John A. Atkins that Hemingway becomes a mystic against his will because the only complete realization of communion lies in death.[48] While Santiago will die soon enough he experiences communion after he harpoons the marlin and eats of its flesh. Manolin has faith in Santiago, and Santiago, as a former champion, is in turn inspired and strengthened whenever he thinks of the great Joe DiMaggio. This communion of champions reinforces Santiago's above-discussed communion with the fish and Manolin. It is the mystique of the champions who "have faith" in themselves and in others like them. We sense that Manolin will also become a champion; that he too will in time be "destroyed" by old age but not "defeated."

Joe DiMaggio, the great baseball player, is a champion. Because he beat the Negro from Cienfuegos in the hand-wrestling match, Santiago is also known as a champion. DiMaggio's father, who was a fisherman, is by virtue of this fact "related" to Santiago, the fisherman, and, by extension to Saint James, the fisherman. "You were born to be a fisherman," says Santiago to himself, "as the fish was born to be a fish. San Pedro was a fisherman as was the father of the great DiMaggio" (p. 105).

DiMaggio's heel spur relates him to Jacob, meaning "of the heel" (Jacob is a variant of James). This makes of him a brother to Santiago. All champions in this novel are in a sense brothers linked to the marlin and, by symbolic extension, to Christ—to all those who struggle against great odds in order to manifest their special abilities. Hemingway sets up a family of champions who are related one to another by strength, suffering, endurance, and will power. The greatest and noblest of all, according to Santiago, is the marlin whose "sword was as long as a baseball bat" (p. 62).

Santiago is a fisherman, Saint James was a fisherman, and Christ was a "fisher of men." All these people will have suffered in one way or another and Santiago imagines DiMaggio, with his bone spur, to be suffering as much as anyone: "What is a bone spur? he asked himself. *Un espuela dé hueso.* We do not have them. Can it be as painful as the spur of a fighting cock in one's heel? I do not think I could endure that" (p. 68). In Spanish *espuela* means not only spur but *spike.* That Santiago's imagination should evoke the image of a fighting cock is significant, since with cock fights, contrary to the "turn the other cheek" of Christianity, it is a fight to the finish. For the reader, however, given the Christ motif, a spike in the foot has its own meaning and again evokes the Crucifixion, an association consonant with popular Spanish religious paintings of the Crucifixion that also frequently depict a cock. Once more Hemingway is using poetic ambiguity. The two themes of the book, the pagan and the Christian, are contained in the same word, *espuela.* Santiago's reaction is a pagan one—the reader's Christian. It is clear that the two themes of the book, and Hemingway's intention in writing it, depend on the necessary distinction between these two points of view.

iii

The pride theme of *The Old Man and the Sea* is developed on two levels: directly, as we have seen, through dialogue and narrative description, and indirectly through symbolic associations. Santiago, as a number of commentators have noted, is the Spanish equivalent of Saint James.* Santiago is also the patron saint of Spain. Santiago, our Cuban fisherman, was born in Spain and to be Spanish, Hemingway informs us in *Death in the Afternoon,* is rather special: "If the people of Spain have one common trait it is pride," and for emphasis: "Pride is the strongest characteristic of the race." But pride, as Hemingway himself has stated, "is a Christian sin and a pagan virtue."⁴⁹ In *The Song of Roland* pride is the cause of the hero's death. Lucifer also fell because of pride. Pride we are told is the most grievous Christian sin. In fact pride, as a challenge to God's or Nature's omniscience, seldom goes unchallenged in return.

Certain proud men, however, like Hemingway and Santiago, feel the need to heighten their sense of manhood by confronting forces that seem bent on their destruction. If you are proud of your self-hood and all of nature conspires to do you in, then it is important that you defend yourself or the concept of man, as Hemingway the ham actor, but also the tragic actor, seems to have done dramatically up to the end. In this context, his suicide takes on particular meaning. If killing fish and animals is to usurp one of God's prerogatives, then the taking of one's own life is an even greater usurpation and challenge to the Deity, as Kiriloff demonstrates in *The Possessed,* with his philosophical suicide. Hemingway's suicide then emerges as an act of defiance which seems to say that he, the man-god, is in control of his destiny and that he will accept no others meddling with his fate. Throughout his entire writing career Hemingway wanted to "survive." But at the end, physically debilitated by his accidents and apparently unable to continue writing in accordance with the high standards he had always set for himself, he seems to have decided that it was time to die. Yet his suicide should perhaps be viewed less as an act of cowardice or despair, than as an act of vengeance against life for having produced a god-like yet mortal being. Unlike Pascal's "bet" for God, Hemingway's suicide looks more like a gamble *against* God. Santiago also "gambles" by going far out in order to defend his identity

---

*Robert M. Brown is perhaps the first to have noted the point. Melvin Backman feels there is an intentional link between the old man and "the fisherman, apostle, and martyr from the Sea of Galilee." See "The Matador and the Crucified." Earl Rovit also notes that "Santiago (St. James) was one of the Disciples of Christ." See "The Structures of the Fiction" in *Ernest Hemingway,* pp. 90–91. Charles K. Hofling notes that Saint James the Apostle was a fisherman and a "fisher of men." See "*The Old Man and the Sea* and the Male Reader," p. 162.

as a fisherman on the one hand and his honor as a man on the other. "Honor to a Spaniard," says Hemingway, "is as real a thing as water, wine, or olive oil." It is something tangible, even palpable.*

If Santiago has lost everything (youth, wife, luck) but his *pundonor* and the lions are the main thing he has left and all that he dreams of, then we have to equate *pundonor* with lions. Do we not think of lions as proud, courageous beasts of the jungle? Do not dreams, as a metaphorical language, when deciphered, reflect the longings, anxieties, and attitudes toward self of the dreamer? Since Santiago's young lions are playful creatures must we not assume that he is on familiar terms with them? "Why are the lions the main thing that is left?" (p. 66). Why indeed! This is an editorial question Hemingway leaves unanswered and which commentators have responded to in different ways. Philip Young feels that to pin down the meaning of the lions and perhaps to answer the question would be to decrease, "vulgarly and gratuitously," the evocative power of their image.[50] We must, however, at the risk of being vulgar and gratuitous, relate Santiago's question to the driving force behind his acts. I suggest that the lions are the very image of his pride.

"The old man was dreaming about the lions" is the last (hence significant) line of the novel. Santiago is lying face down, destroyed physically, but not defeated morally because his ordeal has proved to everyone, particularly to himself, that he is still The Champion. He has demonstrated the ultimate in *pundonor*. It is perhaps difficult to agree with Clinton S. Burhans, Jr., that the lions suggest solidarity and love and humility *as opposed* to individualism and pride, or with Claire Rosenfield that Santiago is broken in spirit. The sharks may have taken his marlin, but he still has his lions, the only thing besides places that he now still dreams of.[51]

Carlos Baker, Sheridan W. Baker, Jackson J. Benson, Bickford Sylvester, Keiichi Harada, and Robert O. Stephens relate the lions to Santiago's past, to his happiness, and to his diminished confidence. The lions, like Joe DiMaggio, do in fact lend strength and courage to Santiago during his three-day ordeal. These commentators believe

---

*The Spanish word is *pundonor* and "means honor, probity, courage, self-respect and pride in one word." *Death in the Afternoon*, pp. 91–92. In 1934 Hemingway noted several dozen things he loved and loved to do. Relevant to *The Old Man and the Sea* we find *courage, pride, fishing, the Gulf Stream*, and *Santiago de Compostela*. As listed by Carlos Baker in *Hemingway: A Life Story*, p. 261.

.that Santiago is supported by the memory of his youth and the vigor of his past achievements.[52] More specifically, Arvin R. Wells says that the lions "suggest an achieved intimacy between the old man and the proud and often fierce heart of nature that for him is the repository of values."[53] These interpretations seem to me sound and relevant. But if dreaming of the past is all Santiago has left, as some of these commentaries imply, Santiago could indulge in his favorite pastime most comfortably by sleeping in his shack. The fact is that he does not content himself with the role of the impotent old dreamer immersed in his past glory.

Finally, on the question of pride, Hemingway the African hunter knew that a family of lions is called a "pride." Can we not imagine him punning on this word and archetypal image and, as poets do, play on its ambiguity and ambivalence with all the precision which characterizes his writing? To equate a pride of lions with Santiago's inner pride not only answers the question which was left unanswered ("Why are the lions the main thing that is left?"), it also gives the novel, in addition to the biblical resonance, a deeper tragic level.

If we extend the Christ motif to include the lions we are reminded that Christ is "the great, mighty, and invincible lion of the tribe of Judah" (Rev. 5:5) and that the line of Boaz, Jesse, and David which produced Jesus is of that tribe (Luke 3:30). The name Santiago is also of "that tribe" since Santiago is the Spanish for Saint James. We remember that one of the Jameses referred to in the Bible is Christ's brother and that throughout the narrative Santiago keeps calling the fish his "brother." The word "brother" works on the naturalistic level as well as on the symbolic Christian level, thus adding to the poetic ambiguity.

iv

The Old Man and the Sea is a poem built on linguistic ambivalence, association, resonance, and knowledge. "There are many tricks" that allow us to catch fish, says Santiago (p. 14) and, had he been a writer, he might have added, tricks of the language, legitimate in themselves and not to be discounted—tricks which make it possible to amplify the meaning of a work of art.

On the realistic level Santiago is no more than an old Cuban fisherman. Yet the novel is so fraught with christological imagery that Hemingway, for all his denials of intentional symbolism invites the reader to ponder the meaning of every name and every association. John Halverson phrases it nicely when he says that "we are virtually required to extend the meaning beyond the particularity of the story's persons and places."[54]

However, a demonstration of symbolic resonance will succeed only if we keep in mind the simultaneity of Hemingway's artistic process, i.e., the blending and overlapping of narrative, theme, symbolism, and fourth or fifth dimensions.* "I always try to write on the principle of the iceberg," said Hemingway in an interview. "There is seven-eighths of it underwater for every part that shows."[55] Everything relates to everything else and it is impossible not to bring in the complexity and prolixity, width and depth of that iceberg below the surface.

Commentators like D. S. Savage and Leon Edel have criticized Hemingway for his superficiality, but if the iceberg theory works then we have to agree with Philip Young, Malcolm Cowley, Carlos Baker and many others who insist that Hemingway's stylistic directness and apparent simplicity hide a rich, inner, symbolic imagery. Baker goes so far as to say that "once the reader has become aware of what Hemingway is doing in those parts of his work which lie below the surface, he is likely to find symbols operating everywhere."[56] Hemingway himself, while disclaiming the conscious use of symbolism, leaves the door open for symbolic interpretations of his

---

*See *Green Hills of Africa* (pp. 26-27). The fifth dimension is perhaps the domain of moral insight while the fourth dimension may be the realm of esthetic experience. In any case, Hemingway forces language and prose to become poetry. W. M. Frohock in "Mr. Hemingway's Truly Tragic Bones," pp. 74-75, says that to call *The Old Man and the Sea* a novel is a confusion of terms. "It comes closer to being a poem." Frohock sees Hemingway as less concerned with human relations than with his own relationship to the universe—"a concern which might have spontaneously flowered into poetry." Harry Levin in "Observations on the Style of Ernest Hemingway," in *Hemingway,* edited by Robert P. Weeks, p. 85, reminds us that Hemingway was not a novelist by vocation, "that he was—and still is—a poet." See F. I. Carpenter in "Hemingway Achieves the Fifth Dimension," in *Hemingway and His Critics,* edited by Carlos Baker, pp. 192-201. See William J. Handy in "A New Dimension for a Hero: Santiago of *The Old Man and the Sea,*" in *Six Contemporary Novels,* edited by William O. S. Sutherland, Jr., p. 68. See also Sam S. Baskett in "Toward a 'Fifth Dimension' in *The Old Man and the Sea,*" pp. 269-86.

work.* Bernard Berenson believes that every work of art, including *The Old Man and the Sea,* "exhales symbols and allegories."[57]

Hemingway once said that knowledge is what makes the underwater part of the iceberg. And he adds that if he had not eliminated everything unnecessary to conveying experience to the reader, *The Old Man and the Sea* would have been over a thousand pages long.†
In keeping with this formula, Hemingway's novel gives the reader only the sketchiest information on Cuba or the Bible, yet Hemingway's knowledge of both was profound. For instance, Santiago promises to make a pilgrimage to the shrine of the Virgin of Cobre if she will help him catch the fish. If we look for extrinsic information which is only hinted at and never elaborated, we learn that the Virgin of Cobre was a mulatto virgin who appeared in a vision to some Cuban fishermen off the coast of Cuba near the Cobre copper mines. She subsequently became the patron saint of Cuba and of Cuban fishermen and, appropriately, her picture hangs in Santiago's shack even though it once belonged to and is a reminder of his wife. A shrine exists

---

*"No good book has ever been written that has in it symbols arrived at beforehand and stuck in. That kind of symbol sticks out like raisins in raisin bread. Raisin bread is all right, but plain bread is better." In *The Old Man and the Sea* "I tried to make a real old man, a real boy, a real sea and a real fish and real sharks. But if I made them good and true enough they would mean many things." *Time* 64 (December 13, 1954): 72.

†See Plimpton, p. 84. Knowledgeable ingredients that went into the composition of *The Old Man and the Sea* include a lifetime of experience. Hemingway, the fisherman, boatman, navigator, and onetime resident of the Florida Keys and Cuba knew the Gulf Stream, the Cuban fishermen, and the habits of big fish. In *To Have and Have Not,* Hemingway describes, among other adventures, the errors one man makes in trying to land a big one. There is also the remarkable story of an aged fisherman who had fought a marlin on the Gulf Stream for several days only to lose it to the sharks. In 1936 Hemingway wrote an account of this episode which he published in the April issue of *Esquire* (pp. 31, 184–85), entitled "On the Blue Water": "an old man fishing alone in a skiff out of Cabañas hooked a great marlin that, on the heavy sashcord handline, pulled the skiff far out to sea. Two days later the old man was picked up by fishermen 60 miles to the eastward, the head and the forward part of the marlin lashed alongside. What was left of the fish, less than half, weighed 800 pounds. The old man had stayed with him a day, a night, a day and another night while the fish swam deep and pulled the boat. When he had come up the old man had pulled the boat up on him and harpooned him. Lashed alongside the sharks had hit him and the old man had fought them out alone in the Gulf Stream in a skiff, clubbing them, stabbing at them, lunging at them with an oar until he was exhausted and the sharks had eaten all they could hold. He was crying in the boat when the fishermen picked him up, half crazy from his loss, and the sharks were still circling the boat."

approximately three hundred miles from Havana to commemorate the miracle. Though Cubans are probably the only ones to bring knowledge of these details to a reading of the novel, the experience is universal because all Catholics can understand Santiago's promise. At the climax of his fight with the sharks he "could hardly breathe now and he felt a strange taste in his mouth. It was *coppery* [my emphasis] and sweet and he was afraid of it for a moment" (p. 119). Something breaks in his chest and he spits blood. A number of commentators have argued, logically it seems to me, that this is Santiago's final hour and though he is dying, his heart, like the giant turtle's, will continue to beat for hours (p. 37). If we accept this reading, then the Virgin of Cobre, the coppery taste in Santiago's mouth, and the prayer he addresses to her (since cobre in Spanish means copper) have an ironic association: "Holy Mary, Mother of God, pray for us sinners now and at the hour of our death. Amen" (p. 65).

The interdependence of poetic ambiguity, ironic treatment of death, and extrinsic biblical knowledge applies also to the resonance of the name Santiago. James, in turn, is a variant of Jacob, and Jacob, as we know, was Jake's name in *The Sun Also Rises.* According to Genesis 25:19-26, Abraham was the father of Isaac, and Isaac was forty years old when he married Rebekah. "And Isaac prayed to the Lord for his wife, because she was barren; and the Lord granted his prayer, and Rebekah his wife conceived." It is an irony perhaps that Santiago's barren luck does not prompt him to pray but to gamble on a lottery ticket. Genesis also tells us that Rebekah's children struggle within her and "When her days to be delivered were fulfilled, behold, there were twins in her womb. The first came forth red, all his body like a hairy mantle; so they called his name Esau. Afterward his brother came forth, and his hand had taken hold of Esau's heel; so his name was called Jacob" (meaning "by the heel"). Because he took his brother's place and is the father of the founders of the twelve tribes of Israel, Jacob is known as the "supplanter."[58]

We have Jacob and Esau, Santiago and the marlin, two "brothers" divided yet held together by the fisherman's cord: God's purpose for Israel and Christianity, man's purpose for Hemingway's naturalistic humanism. Symbol hunters will be tempted (though this writer has reservations about pushing such symbolism to its outer limits) to conclude that Hemingway wants Santiago's "message" to "supplant" Christ's, as Jacob "supplanted" his brother Esau. Jacob is on the one hand he who "supplants" and on the other he who "overreaches"—qualities which are both applicable to Santiago—the realistic fisherman and symbolic patriarch. "Read anything I write for the pleasure of reading it," says Hemingway. "Whatever else you find will be the measure of what you brought to the reading."[59]

If we bring a more detailed reading of the Bible to *The Old Man and the Sea* we also learn that there were three Jameses (some commentaries list four), one of whom was known as James the Greater, the son of Zebedee and brother of the Apostle John. He was originally a fisherman who was called to be a disciple of Jesus and an apostle. He was killed by Herod Agrippa in 44 A.D. and is the only apostle whose death is recorded in the Scriptures. One legend has him travelling and preaching in Spain while another says that his body was miraculously carried to Compostela where his bones were laid to rest.[60]

Another legend says that the body of James the Greater, after his martyrdom in Palestine, was brought to Spain and landed at Padron, one of the ports of Santiago. Padron boasts two great stones called *Barca* and *Patron* (the ship and the skipper), apparent allusions to Saint James the fisherman—associations fully relevant to *The Old Man and the Sea*. After the Moorish conquest, the northwest corner of Spain was the only part of the country that retained its independence. It was from this region that the reconquest of Spain for Christendom was begun, hence the importance of the shrine at Santiago de Compostela.[61] Since James the Greater is the patron saint of Spain, and since Santiago, the Cuban fisherman, bears his name, the old man would seem to represent the crest of the iceberg and thus carry the entire Spanish and Christian legacy with him—a legacy which, with bullfighting and Catholicism, is simultaneously pagan and Christian. The dual theme of the book is artistically consistent with the choice of names.

Santiago is not only Spain's patron saint, he also has cities, provinces, rivers, capes, mountains, and islands named after him in Bolivia, Brazil, Chile, the Dominican Republic, Mexico, Panama, Paraguay, the Philippines, Spain, Puerto Rico, Texas, California, Peru, Cuba, Argentina, and Ecuador. Santiago is a very popular and very important saint in the Spanish-speaking world. His name bears silent witness to the conquest of Latin America for Christendom. Santiago carries his "weight" to the continents through centuries of tradition. Because of such prestigious backing, the old fisherman who has gone for eighty-four days without catching a fish might well, like the biblical Saul, ask himself why God has forsaken him.

Another James, known as James the Less, is identified as one of Christ's brothers (Mark 6:3). He is also known as Saint James the Apostle, one of a very special group within the twelve which was particularly close to Christ. This James was always present on great occasions, e.g., the raising of Jairus's daughter (Mark 5:37), the transfiguration (Mark 9:1) and the agony in the garden (Mark 15:33). According to Acts 12:2, James suffered martyrdom about fourteen years after the death of Christ. This James is thought to be the son of Zebedee and Salome, the sister of Mary, the mother of Jesus, which would make him Christ's cousin. But the Helvidian theory, as propounded by Helvidius and apparently accepted by Tertullian, favors this James as Christ's brother. To some scholars this kinship seems more in keeping with the statements of the Gospels and also with the after-history of the brothers.[62] Therefore, when the old man of the sea calls the fish his "brother" we have not only nature's interrelatedness to keep in mind but also historical "facts" which corroborate an extrinsic reading of the novel.

James (Christ's brother, not the cousin—Matt. 13:55; Mark 6:3) was apparently the eldest of three. He was called the "just," undertook long intercessions for the people, and was martyred by the scribes and Pharisees.[63] *The Biblical Expositor,* however, views James, the son of Joseph and Mary, as only Christ's half-brother. Whatever differences of opinion may exist as to their kinship, James has been accredited historically by the Christian Church as the author of the New Testament "Epistle" which bears his name.[64]

"The Epistle of James," according to the *Dartmouth Bible,*[65] is a vigorous homily written in the form of a letter. It is a guide for daily living that presents Christianity less as a religion of "faith" than one of "attainment" or of "works." While the "Epistle" is considered very modern due to its interest in democracy, philanthropy, and social justice,[66] it is known primarily for its five main themes which bear an uncanny resemblance to the themes of *The Old Man and the Sea:* 1) Endurance under trial; 2) The superiority of deeds to theory; 3) Just dealings with the poor; 4) The perils of evil speech; 5) The need for humility and sincerity.

"Blessed is the man who endures trial," says the letter of James (1:12), words which find an echo in commentators' allusions to

Santiago's "grace under pressure." The old man's endurance is in fact one of Hemingway's most carefully developed themes. Santiago hooks the marlin at noon of the first day. "Then he rested against the bow . . . tried not to think but only to endure" (p. 46). The fish makes a surge that pulls him down on his face and makes a cut below his eye, but Santiago vows to stay with the fish until he is dead (p. 52). Soon the old man's back stiffens and begins to hurt and his hand begins to bleed (pp. 55, 56). His cramped left hand becomes "a claw" and "almost as stiff as rigor mortis" (pp. 58–59). He is alone at sea and out of sight of land. His left hand uncramps at noon on the following day but he is too tired even to pray (pp. 64–65). The ache from the cord across his back has gone beyond pain "into a dullness that he mistrusted" (p. 74). The line cuts his hands. He endures without sleep, at first, then manages to sleep briefly thus making it possible to hold onto the fish for three days. By this time "the old man was wet with sweat and tired deep into his bones" (p. 87). The sweat salts his eyes and the cut above his eye. He sees black spots in front of his eyes and feels faint and dizzy. As the marlin begins to circle at noon of the third day Santiago is more tired than he has ever been in his life (p. 89), yet he forces the great fish to circle at least fourteen times. "I'll try again, the old man promised, although his hands were mushy now and he could only see well in flashes" (p. 93). Somehow he musters the strength to kill the fish, lashes it to his skiff and fights sharks all the way back to Havana. "Fight them," he said. "I'll fight them until I die" (p. 115). He kills sharks with his harpoon, his knife, his oars, and the tiller, even in the dark, until he spits blood from his lungs. Then "he knew he was beaten" (p. 119).

If Santiago is beaten it is only because his body has failed, not his will to endure. His determination does not waver. "Pain does not matter to a man," he says (p. 84). This endurance under trial proves not only the superiority of man to animals but also the superiority of deeds to theory. He who perseveres, says the "Epistle" (1:25), "being no hearer that forgets but a doer that acts, he shall be blessed in his doing." The first and second themes of the "Epistle of James" are in fact the backbone of Hemingway's novel. "God help me endure," says Santiago. "I'll say a hundred Our Fathers and a hundred Hail Marys. But I cannot say them now. Consider them said, he thought. I'll say them later" (p. 87). It is skill and endurance that catch the fish. James wrote not about Christianity's mystical or philosophical aspects but about its practical, every-day aspects. The "Epistle's" purpose was to recall Christians from their worldliness and from their misconceptions of Christianity to the moral *acts* of their faith.[67]

According to Santiago, he and the boy Manolin are the only ones who still have "faith." Santiago scorns the other fishermen who have gone modern—who use outboard motors instead of oars—particularly the rich who have radios and are crazy and do not care for the poor (p. 39). Yet it is the poor of the village who have retained an altruistic ethic, for they fish, endure, and help each other as Manolin helps the old man. The poor are the living example of just dealings with each other—this being the third theme of James's letter.

The fourth theme of the "Epistle," dealing with the perils of evil speech, might better be phrased as a corollary, i.e., the virtues of good speech or the power of auto-suggestion. Throughout the ordeal Santiago talks to himself, bracing himself with words. During moments of particular stress he talks to his left hand, he talks to the fish, he talks to himself about his victory over the great Negro from Cienfuegos—a contest which lasted twenty-four hours and which in itself was a memorable test of endurance. As Santiago tries to pull in the marlin he tells his legs to hold up and last and his head to remain clear. "I am not good for many more turns. Yes you are, he told himself. You're good for ever" (p. 92).

The fifth theme, stressing humility and sincerity, is perhaps more difficult to assimilate insomuch as pride, the main theme of this study, would seem to contradict it. But I see no contradiction in being ambivalent about the forces of nature, awed by them on the one hand and moved to challenge them on the other. "Man is not much beside the great birds and beasts," says Santiago (p. 68). Yet he takes great pride in being a man and in vanquishing the marlin—the noblest of them all. I see pride as the touchstone for his sincerity: humble in the face of nature yet part of nature and responsive to her laws. It is not only strength and endurance that matter, these being the attributes of nature's noblest creatures, but also human attributes of intelligence and will. If there is humility involved it is a humility of strength and the sincerity to affirm it as a manifestation of man's pride. Nor is such pride inconsistent with feelings of remorse. "I shouldn't have gone out so far, fish," he said. "Neither for you nor for me. I'm sorry, fish" (p. 110).

In addition to the five main themes of the "Epistle" discussed

so far, James's reproach to "unfaithful spouses" should also be mentioned. Santiago has not remarried though his wife has been dead for
many years. There is also the curious episode of the male marlin which
remains with the female after she has been hooked and gaffed. Robert P.
Weeks says that Santiago's story of the devoted male marlin "is a pre-
posterous piece of natural history, combining sentimentality and
inexact observation."[68] While dissection may be the only way of telling
a male and female marlin apart, Santiago's remembrance of the faith-
fulness of the male to the female fits into the parallelism with the
"Epistle of James." The "fakery" Weeks speaks of applies to the realistic level, not the symbolic. The male marlin "was beautiful . . . and
he had stayed" (p. 50). This is perhaps, as Carlos Baker claims, an
example of "gallantry against gallantry" but, we might add, one of
fidelity as well. The moral lesson that Hemingway is conveying, even
with this "faked" example, is that nature is the best guide and
teacher. The six-point parallelism with Saint James's letter is not
Hemingway's apologia for Christianity, but a treatise on the superiority
of natural law. The God-fish that Hemingway and Santiago slay is a
tradition that, according to Hemingway's canon, might better be
replaced by the eternal verities of life and death and struggle on the
open sea. James's letter is an exhortation to Christians to behave as
Christians whereas Santiago's "message" is for man alone in contact
with nature and himself. The "Epistle" was written for men who live
in groups whereas Santiago's moral example teaches men everywhere
a lesson of ethical fortitude and stoicism—one which has to be faced
and learned alone.

"Count it all joy, my brethren, when you meet various trials, for
you know that the testing of your faith produces steadfastness" (James
1:2-3). According to James it is man's deeds and endurance that
demonstrate his faith in the new Christianity. Santiago demonstrates
faith well enough, but it is a faith in himself and in the superiority of
man.

v

This pride—in self, and in Santiago's case in being a fisherman
(which is what he "was born for")—and his eighty-four fishless days and
recent loss of public esteem, prompt him on the eighty-fifth day to

gamble with his luck and go out "too far." He also decides to gamble on a lottery ticket which must contain the number eighty-five. Why eighty-five?

Robert N. Broadus[69] writes that Zane Grey, in his *Adventures in Fishing,*[70] complains about his long and unparalleled streak of blankety-blank days. "I had caught my last fish around August 22. Here was a stretch of eighty-three days without catching a fish. I know quite well it cannot be beaten. There is a record that will stand." Broadus suggests that Hemingway could not resist bettering by one day the fishless record set by Zane Grey. This explanation is plausible, since Hemingway, the great fisherman, had probably read or heard about Grey's extended trip to Tahitian waters in 1928. Broadus, however, says nothing about Santiago's previous record of eighty-seven fishless days. Moreover, Zane Grey's record, while it may have anecdotal interest, unlike the Christ motif, has no intrinsic or extrinsic value for the novel.

John Halverson has come up with another ingenious explanation for the choice of eighty-five which has to do with the number of days from Christmas to Easter.[71] According to his calculations, 1951, the year Hemingway was writing the novel, corresponds almost exactly to the religious calendar commemorating the life of Christ from the Nativity to Easter. Events such as carrying the mast up the hill, falling under its weight, and collapsing in a cruciform position, says Halverson, allude to the events of Good Friday. In 1951 Good Friday was the eighty-ninth day from Christmas. Halverson says that Santiago's homecoming takes place on the eighty-eighth day of the novel's calendar and suggests that Hemingway's math may be responsible for the discrepancy.

We know that Santiago hooks the marlin at noon on the eighty-fifth day and harpoons him at noon on the eighty-eighth, three days later. No exact time is specified for his return to the fishing village outside Havana, but when he sails into the little harbour the lights of the Terrace are out and "he knew everyone was in bed" (p. 120). The Terrace, as we know, is frequented by tourists and it would have to be pretty late for them to be in bed. Santiago's return occurs after midnight on the eighty-ninth day since at midnight he is still fighting sharks (p. 118). This means that Hemingway's "calculations" were correct and Santiago's homecoming and "crucifixion" do correspond to Good Friday of the year 1951. It is certainly conceivable that Hemingway took advantage of such a happy numerical coincidence.

While Halverson neatly explains the eighty-nine days that Hemingway the author bends to his advantage, we are still left to ponder why Santiago thinks eighty-five will be his lucky number (p. 16).

Eighty-five is Santiago's choice of numbers and represents his point of view, while eighty-nine, if Halverson's hypothesis is correct, represents Hemingway's. Santiago expects to catch his fish and bring it back on the same day and has no inkling that his author will extend the ordeal three more days in order to have it coincide with Good Friday of 1951. I would suggest that the number eighty-five allows for two additional hypotheses, none of which has yet been commented on.

The first of these extrinsic possibilities may be Hemingway's tribute to Carlos Gutiérrez, the man after whom Santiago was modeled. Gutiérrez began going to sea with his father in 1884 when he was six. He fished with a handline using baits cunningly lashed at various depths (just like Santiago) and was known several times in the past fifteen years to have boated more marlin than any other commercial fisherman working out of Casablanca.[72] Hemingway may simply have extrapolated the number eighty-four in memory of this great fisherman who, after his initiation in 1884, became in every sense of the word a Champion.

The second explanation is both intrinsic and extrinsic and depends on the resonance and associations evoked by the name Santiago. When you add San or Sant (Saint) to the Spanish Iago it becomes Santiago. If we relate Iago and Jacob the Hebrew patriarch, second son of Isaac and father of the founders of the twelve tribes of Israel, to the fact that today the shaft of Jacob's Well is eighty-five feet deep,* then look at the text of the novel, we see that by page forty-one "eighty-five days" has been repeated five times.

Santiago "worked the deep wells for a week and did nothing" (p. 30). If fish are so plentiful in the wells and, as we know, God provides for his own, why has Santiago not caught any? Has he fallen so far out of favor with God and luck that he must in the future rely exclusively on himself? Apparently, since he is *salao*. So, on the eighty-fifth day he decides not to fish the wells, but to go far out where other men do

---

*Miller, p. 300. In ancient times Jacob's Well was quite deep. Today, depending on the biblical dictionary consulted, the depth is variously estimated at between 75 and 125 feet.

not venture. Why? One reason is that the wells have yielded no fish, but on another level, Hemingway's "quarrel with God" and Santiago's "challenge" prompt them to rely exclusively on their own abilities. Accordingly Santiago baits four hooks at forty, seventy-five, one hundred, and one hundred and twenty-five feet. The first depth, forty, like a code, gives the biblical motif. As for the others, is it pure coincidence that different biblical dictionaries record the present depth of Jacob's well at seventy-five, eighty-five, one hundred, and one hundred and twenty-five feet, numbers which correspond to the depth of Santiago's "precise" lines and the chosen lucky day?

Hemingway, the artist, seems to have overextended himself to prove once more that he is the greatest writer while Santiago, the fisherman, brings back an eighteen foot skeleton of a marlin to show that he is still the best. It is an irony that this Spanish Jacob, whose biblical name is sometimes interpreted to mean "he overreaches,"[73] should catch the largest fish, not in the wells where his name and expectation would suggest, but out on the Gulf Stream where he can rely not on tradition, but only on his skill, intelligence, endurance, and will power.

Paul Valéry has recorded his reaction to a Sorbonne exegesis of *Le Cimetière marin* by a professor friend. Valéry noted his ambivalent pleasure and perplexity at the interpretations and meanings of lines and stanzas which he had not consciously intended yet which now, based on the text, seemed to him both logical and tenable. And so it is with all art which, if it is great, will always contain more than meets the eye. Hemingway even believed that certain kinds of knowledge were, in a Jungian sense, part of every man's collective unconscious and were therefore capable of giving us intuitive insight and understanding of relationships which we would not otherwise have access to.*

In conclusion, *The Old Man and the Sea* is a long prose poem that has to be read on several simultaneous levels: the realistic and the symbolic, the intrinsic and the extrinsic. Hemingway's writing produces a series of associations based on linguistic ambiguity and symbolic

---

*Hemingway: "A writer, if he is any good, does not describe. He invents or *makes* out of knowledge personal and impersonal and sometimes he seems to have unexplained knowledge which could come from forgotten racial or family experience. Who teaches the homing pigeon to fly as he does; where does a fighting bull get his bravery, or a hunting-dog his nose?" As quoted by Plimpton, p. 85.

vibrations that give the reader a certain feeling about the work. These ineffable, undefinable, and intangible reactions to Santiago and the Christ motif combine to give an emotional impact that is a blend of the writer's skill, the reader's intuition, and his knowledge. The novel's realism constitutes one eighth of the iceberg. Seven eighths are underwater. Together they produce a "fourth" and "fifth dimension" which, according to Hemingway, come from a prose that has never before been written and which is more difficult than poetry. The combination reveals the inner, invisible dimension of the old man of the sea—his pride—while the narrative voice and slaying of the fish give us a Hemingway who, like Jacob, wrestles with an angel and emerges victorious. The marlin is dead. Long live Manolin.

NOTES

INTRODUCTION

1.   "The Living Gide," *Situations* (New York: George Braziller, Inc., 1965). Originally published in *Les Temps Modernes* 6 (1951): 1537-41.

1. GIDE AND REBELLION

GIDE THE (IM)MORALIST

1.   André Gide, *Dostoievsky* (Paris: Henri Jonquières et Cie, 1928), p. 59. See W. W. Holdheim, *Theory and Practice of the Novel: A Study of André Gide* (Geneva: Droz, 1968); see also H. M. Fayer, *Gide, Freedom and Dostoevsky* (Burlington: Lane Press, 1946).
2.   *Journal*, July 3, 1930. In French: the two-volume Pléiade edition (Paris: Gallimard, 1948, 54). In English: the four-volume Random House edition (New York: 1947-51). The English translations in the text are my own. Subsequent references to the *Journal* appear within the text.
3.   André Gide, *Les Nourritures terrestres* (Paris: Gallimard, Pléiade edition, 1958), p. 157.
4.   See Ben Stoltzfus, "The Protestant Eagle," *Gide's Eagles*, pp. 51-73.
5.   See Henri Peyre's excellent discussion of this topic entitled "André Gide: Martyr and Hero of Sincerity," *Literature and Sincerity*, pp. 276-305.
6.   *Journal 1889-1939* (Paris: Gallimard, Pléiade edition, 1948), p. 1284. See Stoltzfus, "The Catholic Dialogue," *Gide's Eagles*, pp. 73-125.
7.   Albert Camus, the author of *The Rebel*, pays grateful tribute to Gide's influence on him in the special *N.R.F.* edition entitled "Hommage à André Gide," (Paris: Gallimard, 1951), p. 227.
8.   *La Mort d'André Gide* (Paris: Editions Estienne, 1952), pp. 9-10. See "Correspondance André Gide-François Mauriac 1912-1950," *Cahiers André Gide* (Paris: Gallimard, 1971); also Stoltzfus, "La Correspondance Gide-Mauriac, 1912-1950," *Gide et la fonction de la littérature* (Paris: Minard, 1972), pp. 123-40.

9. See *Correspondance Francis Jammes et André Gide, 1893-1938* (Paris: Gallimard, 1948) and *Correspondance Paul Claudel et André Gide, 1899-1926* (Paris: Gallimard, 1949).
10. See *The God That Failed,* ed. Richard Crossman (New York: Harper and Row, 1950).
11. See George I. Brachfeld, *André Gide and the Communist Temptation.*
12. *Journal 1889-1939.* No date listed. Pléiade edition, 1948, p. 902.
13. "Feuillets d'Automne," 1947, *Journal 1939-1949,* Pléiade edition, p. 309. Exact date not listed.
14. Ibid., p. 310. Exact date not listed.
15. See Catharine H. Savage, *André Gide: l'évolution da sa pensée religieuse,* and E. U. Bertalot, *André Gide et l'attente de Dieu.*
16. Letter to Bernard Enginger, quoted in *Journal 1939-1949,* Pléiade edition, pp. 295-96.

NOTEBOOKS OF ANDRÉ WALTER

1. "Lettre à Scheffer," *Oeuvres Complètes,* IV (Paris: Gallimard, 1932-39), p. 616.
2. See Kurt Weinberg, *On Gide's Prométhée: Private Myth and Public Mystification* (Princeton, N. J.: Princeton University Press, 1972).
3. *Journal,* September and October, 1909. Exact date not listed.
4. Once, when asked what he thought of the great nineteenth century French writer, Gide exclaimed: "Hugo, hélas!"
5. *Journal,* La Roque, August, 1893. Exact date not listed. See Jean Delay, "Le Mal d'André Walter," *La Jeunesse d'André Gide,* pp. 481-599, which discusses the etiology of "the double."
6. See Delay.
7. *André Gide par lui-même,* p. 58-64.
8. *Vie d'André Gide,* p. 138.
9. Catharine Savage, "The Ideology of André Walter." Van Meter Ames, *André Gide,* p. 8.
10. *André Gide: The Evolution of an Aesthetic,* p. 24.
11. Ames, p. 8.
12. See Denis de Rougemont, *Comme toi-même.*
13. *The White Notebook* (New York: The Citadel Press, 1965), p. 4. Parenthetical references are to this edition.
14. *Man for Himself* (New York; Toronto: Rinehart and Company, 1947), pp. 143-44.
15. Ibid., p. 158.
16. *Les Cahiers et les poésies d'André Walter* (Paris: Gallimard, 1952), p. 129. Parenthetical references are to this edition. The translations are my own.

SAUL

1. Jean Hytier, *André Gide,* pp. 156-66; R.-M. Albérès, *L'Odyssée d'André Gide,* p. 133; Claude Martin, *André Gide par lui-même,* p. 104; Jean-Jacques Thierry, *Gide* (Paris: Gallimard, 1962), p. 65. Most of *Saul* was written in Rome in the spring of 1898, soon after the completion of *Fruits of the Earth.*
2. *Saül,* in Gide's *Théâtre* (Paris: Gallimard, 1942), p. 94. Parenthetical references are to this edition. The translations are my own.
3. *Oedipe,* p. 272. Published in *Théâtre.*

2. HEMINGWAY'S BATTLE WITH GOD

PRIDE, *THE OLD MAN AND THE SEA*

1. "Hemingway's Ambiguity: Symbolism and Irony," in *Hemingway*, edited by Robert P. Weeks, p. 53.
2. *Ernest Hemingway*, p. viii.
3. "Confiteor Hominem: Ernest Hemingway's Religion of Man," in Weeks, pp. 164-65.
4. "The Look of Religion: Hemingway and Catholicism," *Renascence* 17, no. 2 (Winter 1964), 78-79.
5. "Ernest Hemingway et le catholicisme sceptique," *Esprit* 23 (July 1955), 1130-43.
6. *L'Age du roman américain* (Paris: Editions du Seuil, 1948), p. 176.
7. "Nada, Religion, and Hemingway," topic 12, vol. 6, *New Perspectives in American Literature* (Toronto: University of Toronto Press, 1967).
8. *Ernest Hemingway*, p. viii.
9. Killinger, *Hemingway and the Dead Gods*, p. 80; Stephens, "Hemingway's Old Man and the Iceberg," p. 303; Baker, *Hemingway: The Writer as Artist*, p. 299; Waldmeir, "Confiteor Hominem: Ernest Hemingway's Religion of Man," p. 161; Gurko, *Ernest Hemingway and the Pursuit of Heroism*, p. 159; Burhans, "*The Old Man and the Sea*: Hemingway's Tragic Vision of Man," in *Twentieth Century Interpretations of "The Old Man and the Sea,"* edited by Katharine Jobes, p. 78; Wells, "A Ritual of Transfiguration: *The Old Man and the Sea*," in *Twentieth Century Interpretations of "The Old Man and the Sea,"* p. 62; Young, "*The Old Man and the Sea*: Vision/Revision," in *Twentieth Century Interpretations of "The Old Man and the Sea,"* p. 23; Hovey, *Hemingway: The Inward Terrain*, p. 197.
10. Madeleine S. and J. Lane Miller, *Harper's Bible Dictionary* (New York: Harper and Brothers, 1952), pp. 541-42.
11. (New York: Charles Scribner's Sons, 1952), pp. 124, 126. Subsequent page references to this edition will appear within the body of the text.
12. "Dramatic Structure in the Novels of Ernest Hemingway," *Modern Fiction Studies*, XIV, no. 3 (Autumn 1968), 281.
13. "Hemingway's *The Old Man and the Sea* and the Male Reader," p. 164.
14. *Death in the Afternoon* (New York: Charles Scribner's Sons, 1932), p. 233.
15. "Christian Resonance in *The Old Man and the Sea*," p. 52.
16. Ibid., p. 54.
17. "Hemingway's Tragic Vision of Man," p. 78.
18. *The Inward Terrain*, p. 198.
19. Baker, *The Writer as Artist*, p. 319; Backman, "Hemingway: The Matador and the Crucified," pp. 2-11; d'Agostino, "The Later Hemingway," Weeks, ed., p. 158; Wells, "A Ritual of Transfiguration," pp. 56-63; Young, "Vision/Revision," p. 23; Waldmeir, "Confiteor Hominem," p. 163; Gurko, *Pursuit of Heroism*, p. 159.
20. *The Writer as Artist*, p. 299.
21. *Advertisements for Myself* (New York: Putnam, 1959), p. 19.
22. *Hemingway and the Dead Gods*, p. 64.
23. *Hemingway . . . The Writer's Art of Self-Defense*, p. 130.
24. As quoted by William B. Dillingham, "Hemingway and Death," p. 101.
25. "Hemingway's Ambiguity: Symbolism and Irony," ed. Weeks, pp. 53-54.
26. Quoted by Maxwell Perkins in *Scribner's Magazine* 81, no. 3 (March 1927).
27. "Hemingway's Old Men," p. 35.
28. *Hemingway and the Dead Gods*, pp. 79-80.
29. "Hemingway and Old Age: Santiago as Priest of Time," p. 220.
30. "A New Dimension for a Hero: Santiago of *The Old Man and the Sea*," in *Six Contemporary Novels*, edited by William O. S. Sutherland, Jr., p. 64.

31.   *L'Homme Révolté* (Paris: Gallimard, 1951), p. 41.
32.   Quoted in *Time* 60, no. 9 (September 1, 1952), 48.
33.   *Death in the Afternoon*, p. 24, 87.
34.   Ibid., p. 213.
35.   Ibid., p. 206.
36.   "The Matador and the Crucified," pp. 2–12.
37.   *Death in the Afternoon*, pp. 232–33.
38.   Carlos Baker, *Ernest Hemingway: A Life Story*, pp. viii, 252.
39.   Dillingham, p. 96; Ivan Kashkeen, "Alive in the Midst of Death: Ernest Hemingway," in *Hemingway and His Critics*, edited by Carlos Baker, p. 165; G.-A. Astre, *Hemingway par lui-même* (Paris: Editions de Seuil, 1961), p. 61; Quentin Ritzen, *Hemingway* (Paris: Editions Universitaires, 1962), pp. 101-9.
40.   *Death in the Afternoon*, p. 2.
41.   "Hemingway and Death," p. 98.
42.   *The Writer's Art of Self-Defense*, p. 172.
43.   "Hemingway's Extended Vision: *The Old Man and the Sea*," in *Twentieth Century Interpretations of "The Old Man and the Sea*," pp. 91–92.
44.   *Seven Types of Ambiguity* (New York: Meridian Books, 1958).
45.   Miller, p. 278.
46.   *Ernest Hemingway*, p. 129.
47.   "Hemingway's Tragic Vision of Man," pp. 72–80.
48.   *The Art of Ernest Hemingway*, p. 249.
49.   "Because they have pride they do not mind killing." *Death in the Afternoon*, pp. 91, 233, 264.
50.   "Vision/Revision," p. 21.
51.   Burhans, "Hemingway's Tragic Vision of Man," p. 77; Rosenfield, "New World, Old Myths," in *Twentieth Century Interpretations of "The Old Man and the Sea,"* edited by Katharine Jobes, p. 44.
52.   Carlos Baker, *Hemingway: The Writer as Artist*, pp. 308-9; Sheridan W. Baker, pp. 129-30; Jackson J. Benson, *The Writer's Art of Self-Defense*, p. 125; Bickford Sylvester, "'They Went Through This Fiction Every Day': Informed Illusion in *The Old Man and the Sea*," p. 476; Keiichi Harada, "The Marlin and the Shark: A Note on *The Old Man and the Sea*," in Carlos Baker, *Hemingway and His Critics*, pp. 269-76; Robert O. Stephens, "Hemingway's Old Man and the Iceberg," p. 302.
53.   "A Ritual of Transfiguration," p. 63.
54.   "Christian Resonance," p. 54.
55.   George Plimpton, "Ernest Hemingway: The Art of Fiction," 21, p. 84.
56.   *Hemingway: The Writer as Artist*, p. 117.
57.   As quoted by Carlos Baker in *Ernest Hemingway: A Life Story*, p. 505.
58.   Miller, pp. 298-300.
59.   In Plimpton, p. 76.
60.   *The New Century Cyclopedia of Names*, ed. Clarence L. Barnhart, vol. 2 (New York: Appleton-Century-Crofts, Inc., 1954), p. 2164.
61.   *Encyclopaedia Britannica XIX* (Chicago, London, Toronto, Geneva, Sydney, Tokyo, Manila: William Benton, 1970), p. 1045.
62.   William Patrick, *James, the Lord's Brother* (Edinburgh: T. & T. Clark, 1906), p. 5.
63.   Miller, p. 301.
64.   *The Biblical Expositor*, vol. 3 (Philadelphia: A. J. Holman Co., 1960), p. 408.
65.   Roy B. Chamberlin and Herman Feldman, *The Dartmouth Bible* (Boston: Houghton Mifflin Co., 1950), p. 1140.
66.   Edgar J. Goodspeed, *The Story of the Bible* (Chicago: The University of Chicago Press, 1936), p. 104.
67.   Miller, p. 301.

68.   Robert P. Weeks, "Fakery in *The Old Man and the Sea*," in *Twentieth Century Interpretations of "The Old Man and the Sea,"* p. 37.
69.   "The New Record Set by Hemingway's Old Man," pp. 152–53.
70.   Edited with notes by Ed Zern (New York: Harper, 1952), p. 192.
71.   "Christian Resonance," p. 51.
72.   Carlos Baker, *Ernest Hemingway: A Life Story, p. 228.*
73.   *Interpreter's Dictionary of the Bible,* ed. George A. Buttrick (New York, Nashville: Abingdon Press, 1962), p. 783.

BIBLIOGRAPHY

GIDE AND REBELLION

This selected bibliography of secondary sources places particular emphasis on Gide's religious stance, *The Notebooks of André Walter,* and *Saul.*

Abélard, J. "Quelques Aspects stylistiques de la prédiction implicite dans les *Cahiers d'André Walter." Le Français Moderne* 31 (1963): 269-82.

Albérès, R.-M. "L'Exigence et l'amour du destin: *Saül, Candaule, Philoctète* (1899-1903)." *L'Odyssée d'André Gide.* Paris: Editions Albin Michel, 1951, pp. 129-45.

Ames, Van Meter. "God, Son of Man," and "Christ and Marx," *André Gide.* Norfolk, Connecticut: New Directions, 1947, pp. 78-178.

Angeli, Giovanna. "Le Poésie di André Walter." *Paragone* 242 (1970): 78-95.

Baskin, Wade. Introduction to *The Notebooks of André Walter.* New York: Philosophical Library, 1965, pp. 7-14.

———, trans. *The White Notebook* by André Gide. New York: Philosophical Library, 1964.

Bastide, Roger. "Thèmes gidiens." *Cahiers du Sud* 62 (1966): 256-72.

Batchelor, R. E. "Gide et Unamuno. Sotie ou nivola?" *Nottingham French Studies* 9 (1970): 44-53.

Bertalot, Enrico U. *André Gide et l'attente de Dieu.* Paris: Minard, 1967.

Boisdeffre, Pierre de. "André Walter joue et perd (1889-1891)," *La Vie d'André Gide.* Paris: Hachette, 1970, pp. 121-48.

———. "Les Débuts d'un homme de lettres (1891-1892)," *Adam* (1970), pp. 337-39 and (1972), pp. 29-47.

Brachfeld, George I. *André Gide and the Communist Temptation.* Geneva: Droz, 1959.

Brée, Germaine. "The Early Works," *Gide.* New Brunswick, New Jersey: Rutgers University Press, 1963, pp. 31-42.

———. "Form and Content in Gide." *The French Review* 30 (May 1956): 423-28.

Brulez, Raymond. "Gide en Claudel." *Nieuw Vlaams Tijdschrift* 16 (1963): 761-72.

Bulgin, Kathleen. "Swamp Imagery and the Moral-Esthetic Problem in Gide's Early Works." *The French Review* 45 (1972): 813-18.

Chambers, Leland H. "Gide's Fictional Journals." *Criticism* 10 (1967): 300–12.

Church, D. M. "Structure and Dramatic Technique in *Saül* and *Le Roi Candaule*." *PMLA* 84 (1969): 1639–43.

Delay, Jean. "En Écrivant André Walter." *La Table Ronde* 98 (1956): 9–41.

–––. "Le Mal d'André Walter," *La Jeunesse d'André Gide*. Paris: Gallimard, 1956, pp. 481–599.

Facan, Jacques. "La Jeunesse de Gide ou la lettre et le désir." *Critique* 131 (1958): 291–315.

Gagnebin, Laurent. *André Gide nous interroge: Essai critique sur sa pensée religieuse et morale*. Preface by Gilbert Guisan. Lausanne: Cahiers de la Renaissance vaudoise, 1961.

Gard, Roger Martin du. *Notes sur André Gide*. Paris: Gallimard, 1951, p. 31.

Goodhand, Robert. "The Religious Leitmotif in *L'Immoraliste*." *Romanic Review* 57 (1966): 263–76.

Guerard, Albert J. "The Spiritual Autobiographies." *André Gide*. Cambridge, Massachusetts: Harvard University Press, 1969, pp. 34–93.

Haan, T. "'La Foi tout court remplace la bonne.'" *De Nieuwe Stem* 19 (1964): 179–83.

Heckman, John. "Pascal et Gide." *Symposium* 19 (1965): 5–18.

Hill, Charles G. "André Gide and Blake's *Marriage of Heaven and Hell*." *Comparative Literature Studies* 3 (1966): 21–32.

Hytier, Jean. "Plays," *André Gide*. New York: Doubleday, 1962, pp. 148–80.

Ireland, G. W. "André Walter," *André Gide*. New York: Grove Press, 1963, pp. 5–13.

Kuklova, Frances. "L'Influence de Schopenhauer sur André Gide." *Dissertation Abstracts* 25 (1965): 4702–03 (Fordham).

Kushnir, Slava M. "Rencontres: Gide et Green." *Mosaic* 3 (1970), 74–84.

Lindsay, Marshall. "Time in Gide's Early Fiction." *Symposium* 26 (1972): 39–56.

Mallet, Robert. "Un Certain Aspect de l'esprit de dialogue à travers Gide et Claudel." *Australasian Universities Language and Literature Association Proceedings*, vol. 2 (1964): 51.

–––. "Jammes et Gide à travers leurs oeuvres . . . et leur amitié." *Le Figaro Littéraire* (February 18, 1961), pp. 12–13.

Mankin, Paul A. "Reflections on *Le Retour de l'enfant prodigue*." *Modern Language Journal* 47 (1962): 53–55.

March, Harold. "Emmanuèle and God," *Gide and the Hound of Heaven*. New York: A. S. Barnes and Company, Inc., 1961, pp. 19–47.

Marek, Joseph Camille, "Gide et la vertu." *Dissertation Abstracts* 20 (1960): 3746 (Kentucky).

Marsalet, Maurice. *André Gide l'enchaîné. Bordeaux: Picquot, 1955.*

Martin, Claude, André Gide par lui-même. *"Ecrivains de Toujours."* Paris: Editions du Seuil, 1963.

–––. *La Maturité d'André Gide: De Paludes à l'Immoraliste, 1895–1902*. Paris: Klincksieck, 1977.

Martinet, Edouard. *André Gide: L'Amour et la divinité*. Paris: Attinger, 1931.

McLaren, James C. "Art and Moral Synthesis: Gide's Central Focus." *L'Esprit Créateur* 1 (1961): 3–8.

Merchant, Norris. "The Spiritual Dilemma of André Gide." *The Colorado Quarterly* 7 (1959): 406–23.

Nersoyan, H. J. *André Gide: The Theism of an Atheist*. Syracuse, New York: Syracuse University Press, 1969.

Ormesson, Jean d'. "Gide et Mauriac: *Les frères ennemis*." *Les Nouvelles Littéraires* 6 (May 29, 1971). (Rev. art.)

Peyre, Henri. "André Gide: Martyr and Hero of Sincerity," *Literature and Sincerity*. New Haven, Connecticut: Yale University Press, 1963, pp. 276–305.

Roberts, Christina H. "Gide and Dostoevsky." *Dissertation Abstracts* 31 (1970): 2399A (Toronto).

Romains, Jules. "Gide, le stratège diabolique." *Les Nouvelles Littéraires* (June 8, 1961), pp. 1–2.

Rose, Marilyn Gaddis. "'Emmanuèle'-'Morella': Gide's Poe Affinities." *Texas Studies in Literature and Language* 5 (1963): 127–37.

Rossi, Vinio. "*Les Cahiers d'André Walter:* Ambitions and Realizations"; "The Symbol: Practice and Theory." In *André Gide: The Evolution of an Aesthetic.* New Brunswick, New Jersey: Rutgers University Press, 1967, pp. 17–63.

–––. "From Image to Parable in Gide's Early Works." *Dissertation Abstracts* 25 (1965): 6634 (Columbia).

Rougemont, Denis de. *Comme toi-même.* Paris: Albin Michel, 1961.

San Juan, E., Jr. "The Idea of Gide's Theatre." *The Educational Theatre Journal* 17 (1965): 220–24.

Savage, Catherine Hill. "André Gide et André Walter," *André Gide: L'Évolution de sa pensée religieuse.* Paris: Nizet, 1962, pp. 19–52.

–––. "Gide et la tentation du catholicisme claudélien." *The Kentucky Foreign Language Quarterly* 9 (1962): 97–104.

–––. "The Ideology of André Walter." *L'Esprit Créateur* 1 (1961): 14–20.

Schildt, Göran. "Le Christ immoraliste." In *Gide et l'homme.* Paris: Le Mercure de France, 1949, pp. 65–94.

Schlumberger, Jean. "Frère et soeur," and "Les Cahiers d'André Walter." In *Madeleine et André Gide.* Paris: Gallimard, 1956, pp. 20–40.

–––. "Le Vrai Visage de l'Emmanuèle de Gide." *Le Figaro Littéraire* (June 16, 1956), pp. 1, 5.

Schütz, Robert. "André Gides Stellung zum Theater." *Die Neueren Sprachen* 15 (1966): 486–91.

Stoltzfus, Ben. *Gide's Eagles.* Carbondale, Illinois: Southern Illinois University Press, 1969.

–––. "*Saül:* A Germinating Gide." *The French Review* 39 (1965): 49–56.

Storzer, Gerald H. "*Les Cahiers d'André Walter:* Idea, Emotion, and Dream in the Gidian Novel." *Philological Quarterly* 54 (1975): 647–62.

Thiel, Maria. "La Figure de Saül et sa représentation dans la littérature dramatique française." (Amsterdam: H. J. Paris, 1926).

Vildé-Lot, I. "André Gide et 'l'art d'écrire' d'après les variantes des *Nouvelles terrestres* et de quelques autres oeuvres de jeunesse." *Le Français Moderne* 28 (1960): 259–86; and 39 (1961): 29–42, 121–83, 206–22.

Watson, Graeme. "Gide and the Devil." *The Australian Journal of French Studies* 4 (1968): 86–96.

Zulli, Floyd, Jr. "Gide and Dante." *The French Review* 29 (1955): 9–12.

HEMINGWAY'S BATTLE WITH GOD

A detailed checklist of studies in English of *The Old Man and the Sea.*

Aldridge, John W. *Time to Murder and Create: The Contemporary Novel in Crisis.* New York: David McKay, 1966, pp. 185–91.

Atkins, John A. *The Art of Ernest Hemingway.* London: Spring Books, 1952, pp. 227–30.

88 / BIBLIOGRAPHY

Backman, Melvin. "Hemingway: The Matador and the Crucified," *Modern Fiction Studies* 1 (August 1955): 2-11. Reprinted in corrected version in Baker, ed., *Ernest Hemingway: Critiques of Four Major Novels*, pp. 135-43; and in Baker, ed., *Hemingway and his Critics*, pp. 245-58.

Baker, Carlos. "The Ancient Mariner," in *Hemingway: The Writer as Artist*, 3rd ed. Princeton: Princeton University Press, 1963, pp. 289-329. Section 3 of Chapter 12 reprinted as "The Boy and the Lions" in Jobes, ed., *Twentieth Century Interpretations of "The Old Man and the Sea,"* pp. 27-34.

———. "The Old Man and the Sea." *The Saturday Review* 35 (September 6, 1952): 10-11. Reprinted in Edward C. Wagenknecht, ed., *A Preface to Literature*. New York: Henry Holt and Co., 1954, pp. 341-44.

———. *"The Old Man and the Sea."* In *Ernest Hemingway: A Life Story*. New York: Charles Scribner's Sons, 1969, pp. 501-7. Paperback reprint, New York: Bantam, 1970, pp. 635-44.

———. *Ernest Hemingway: Critiques of Four Major Novels*. Scribner Research Anthologies. New York: Charles Scribner's Sons, 1962. "Part Four: The Old Man and the Sea."
p. 132. Mark Schorer. "With Grace under Pressure."
p. 135. Melvin Backman. "Hemingway: The Matador and the Crucified.
p. 144. Joseph Waldmeir. "Confiteor Hominem: Ernest Hemingway's Religion of Man."
p. 150. Clinton S. Burhans, Jr. *"The Old Man and the Sea:* Hemingway's Tragic Vision of Man."
p. 156. Carlos Baker. "Hemingway's Ancient Mariner."

———, ed. *Hemingway and His Critics: An International Anthology*. New York: Hill and Wang, 1961.

Baker, Sheridan W. *Ernest Hemingway*. American Authors and Critics. New York, Chicago, San Francisco, Toronto, London: Holt, Rinehart and Winston, Inc., 1967, pp. 119-36.

Barbour, James, and Robert Sattelmeyer. "Baseball and Baseball Talk in 'The Old Man and the Sea.'" *Fitzgerald/Hemingway Annual* (1975), 281-87.

Baskett, Sam S. "Toward a 'Fifth Dimension' in *The Old Man and the Sea.*" *The Centennial Review* (Michigan State University, 1975), 269-86.

Beaver, Joseph. "'Technique' in Hemingway," *College English* 14 (March 1953), passim.

Benson, Jackson J. "The Mask of Humble Perfection." In *Hemingway . . . The Writer's Art of Self-Defense*. Minneapolis: University of Minnesota Press, 1969, pp. 169-86.

Bluefarb, Samuel. "The Sea—Mirror and Maker of Character in Fiction and Drama." *English Journal* 48 (December 1959): 501-10.

Bocaz, Sergio H. "'El ingenioso hidalgo Don Quijote de la Mancha' and 'The Old Man and the Sea': A Study of the Symbolic Essence of Man in Cervantes and Hemingway." *Bulletin of the Rocky Mountain Modern Language Association* 25 (1971), 49-54.

Bradford, M. E. "On the Importance of Discovering God: Faulkner and Hemingway's *The Old Man and the Sea.*" *Mississippi Quarterly* 20 (Summer 1967): 158-62.

Braun, Richard E. "Echoes from the Sea: A Hemingway Rubric," *Fitzgerald/ Hemingway Annual* (1974), 201-5.

Broadus, Robert N. "The New Record Set by Hemingway's Old Man." *Notes and Queries* 10 (March 1963), 152-53.

Burhans, Clinton S., Jr. *"The Old Man and the Sea:* Hemingway's Tragic Vision of Man." *American Literature* 31 (January 1960): 446-55. Reprinted in Baker, ed., *Hemingway and His Critics*, pp. 259-68, and *Ernest Hemingway: Critiques of Four Major Novels*, pp. 150-55; and in Jobes, ed.,

Twentieth Century Interpretations of "The Old Man and the Sea," pp. 72–81.

Carpenter, F. I. "Hemingway Achieves the Fifth Dimension." In *Hemingway and His Critics.* Edited by Carlos Baker. New York: Hill and Wang, 1961, pp. 192–201.

Ciholas, Karin N. "Three Modern Parables: A Comparative Study of Gide's *L'Immoraliste,* Mann's *Der Tod in Venedig,* and Hemingway's *The Old Man and the Sea." Dissertation Abstracts International* 33 (1973): 4404A (University of North Carolina, Chapel Hill, Dissertation, 1972).

Clendenning, John. "Hemingway's Gods, Dead and Alive." *Texas Studies in Literature and Language* 3 (Winter 1962): 459–63.

Cook, Walter A. "Role Structure in Content Analysis: A Case Grammar Approach to Literature," in *Meaning: A Common Ground of Linguistics and Literature.* Edited by Don L. F. Nilsen, Proceedings, University of Iowa Conference, April 27-28 (1973). Cedar Falls, Iowa, pp. 179–87.

Cooperman, Stanley. "Hemingway and Old Age: Santiago as Priest of Time." *College English* 27 (December 1965): 215–20.

Corin, Fernand. "Steinbeck and Hemingway: A Study in Literary Economy." *Revue des Langues Vivantes* 24 (1958): 60–75, 153–63.

Cotten, L. "Hemingway's *Old Man and the Sea." Explicator* 11 (March 1953), item 38.

Cotter, Janet M. "*The Old Man and the Sea:* An 'Open' Literary Experience." *English Journal* 51 (October 1962): 459–63.

Cowley, Malcolm. "Hemingway's Novel Has the Rich Simplicity of a Classic." *New York Herald Tribune Book Review* 29 (September 7, 1952): 1, 17.

D'Agostino, Nemi. "The Later Hemingway." Translated by Barbara Melchiori Arnett. *The Sewanee Review* 67 (Summer 1960): 482–93. Reprinted in Weeks, ed., *Hemingway: A Collection of Critical Essays,* pp. 152–60.

Davis, Robert Gorham. "Hemingway's Tragic Fisherman," *The New York Times Book Review* (September 7, 1952), 1, 20.

Davison, Richard A. "Carelessness and the Cincinnati Reds in *The Old Man and the Sea." Notes on Contemporary Literature* 1 (1971): 11–13.

Dillingham, William B. "Hemingway and Death." *The Emory University Quarterly* 19 (Summer 1963): 95–102.

Dupee, F. W. "Hemingway Revealed." *The Kenyon Review* 15 (Winter 1953): 150–53.

Fagan, Edward R. "Teaching Enigmas of *The Old Man and the Sea." English Record* 8 (Autumn 1957): 13–20.

Farquhar, Robin H. "Dramatic Structure in the Novels of Ernest Hemingway." *Modern Fiction Studies* 14 (Autumn 1968): 271–83.

Farrington, S. Kip, Jr. *Fishing with Hemingway and Glassell.* New York: David McKay, 1971.

Fiedler, Leslie A. "Adolescence and Maturity in the American Novel," in *An End to Innocence: Essays on Culture and Politics.* Boston: The Beacon Press, 1955, pp. 191–210.

–––. "Men without Women." In Weeks, ed., *Hemingway: A Collection of Critical Essays,* pp. 86–93.

Flora, Joseph M. "Biblical Allusions in 'The Old Man and the Sea.'" *Studies in Short Fiction* (Newberry College, South Carolina) 10 (1973), 143–47.

Forrey, Robert. "The Old Man and the Fish." *Mainstream* 14 (June 1961): 31–38.

Frohock, W. M. "Mr. Hemingway's Truly Tragic Bones." *Southwest Review* 38 (Winter 1953): 74–77.

Gordon, David. "The Son and the Father: Patterns of Response to Conflict in Hemingway's Fiction." *Literature and Psychology* 16 (1960): 135–36.

Grebstein, Sheldon N. "Hemingway's Craft in *The Old Man and the Sea.*" In *The Fifties: Fiction, Poetry, Drama.* Edited by Warren Frend. DeLand, Florida: Everett/Edwards, 1970, pp. 41-50.

Gurko, Leo. "The Heroic Impulse in *The Old Man and the Sea.*" *English Journal* 44 (October 1955): 377-82. The same article appears under the title "The Old Man and the Sea" in *College English* 17 (October 1955): 11-15. Reprinted in Jobes, ed., *Twentieth Century Interpretations of "The Old Man and the Sea,"* pp. 64-71.

–––. "The Old Man and the Sea." In *Ernest Hemingway and the Pursuit of Heroism.* New York: Thomas Y. Crowell Company, 1968, pp. 159-74.

Hagopian, John V., and Martin Dolch. *Insight I: Analyses of American Literature.* Frankfurt am Main: Hirschgraben-Verlag, 1962, pp. 111-12.

Hale, Nancy. "Hemingway and the Courage to Be." In *The Realities of Fiction.* Boston: Little Brown, 1962, 111-12.

Halliday, E. M. "Hemingway's Ambiguity: Symbolism and Irony." *American Literature* 28 (1956): 1-22. Reprinted in Weeks, ed., *Hemingway: A Collection of Critical Essays,* pp. 52-71.

Halverson, John. "Christian Resonance in *The Old Man and the Sea.*" *English Language Notes* 2 (September 1964): 50-54.

Handy, William J. "A New Dimension for a Hero: Santiago of *The Old Man and the Sea.*" In *Six Contemporary Novels.* Edited by William O. S. Sutherland, Jr. Austin: University of Texas Press, 1962, pp. 58-75.

Harada, Keiichi. "The Marlin and the Shark: A Note on *The Old Man and the Sea.*" *Journal* no. 4 of the College of Literature, Aryama Gakuin University, Tokyo. Reprinted in Baker, ed., *Hemingway and His Critics,* pp. 269-76.

Harlow, Benjamin C. "Some Archetypal Motifs in *The Old Man and the Sea.*" *McNeese Review* (McNeese State College, Louisiana) 17 (1966): 74-79.

Hauger, B. A. "First Person Perspective in Four Hemingway Stories." *Rendezvous* 6 (1971), 29-38.

Heaton, C. P. "Style in *The Old Man and the Sea.*" *Style* 4 (1970): 11-27.

Hemingway, Ernest. "On the Blue Water." *Esquire* (April 1936), pp. 31, 184-85.

Hofling, Charles K., M.D. "Hemingway's *The Old Man and the Sea* and the Male Reader." *American Imago* 20 (Spring 1963): 161-73.

Hotchner, A. E. *Papa Hemingway.* New York: Bantam, 1967. See pp. 78-80.

Hovey, Richard B. "The Last of the Heroes: Novels of the Fifties." In *Hemingway: The Inward Terrain.* Seattle and London: University of Washington Press, 1968, pp. 191-203.

–––. "*The Old Man and the Sea:* A New Hemingway Hero." *Discourse* 9 (Summer 1966): 283-94.

Howard, Milton. "Hemingway and Heroism." *Masses and Mainstream* 5 (October 1952): 1-8.

Isabelle, Julianna. *Hemingway's Religious Experience.* New York: Vantage Press, 1964, pp. 65, 73-74 and passim.

Jobes, Katharine T., ed. *Twentieth Century Interpretations of "The Old Man and the Sea."* Englewood Cliffs, N. J.: Prentice-Hall, Inc., 1968. Introduction by Katharine Jobes, pp. 1-18.

Johnston, Kenneth G. "The Star in Hemingway's *The Old Man and the Sea.*" *American Literature* 42 (1970): 388-91.

Josephs, Mary J. "The Hunting Metaphor in Hemingway and Faulkner." *Dissertation Abstracts International,* 34 (1973), 1282A-83A, Michigan State University.

Kaplan, Harold. "Hemingway and the Passive Hero." In *The Passive Voice: An Approach to Modern Fiction.* Athens, Ohio: Ohio University Press, 1966, pp. 108-10.

Kashkeen, Ivan. "Alive in the Midst of Death: Ernest Hemingway." In *Hemingway and His Critics*. Edited by Carlos Baker. New York: Hill and Wang, 1961, pp. 171–73.

Killinger, John. *Hemingway and the Dead Gods: A Study in Existentialism*. Lexington: University of Kentucky Press, 1960, passim. Reprinted: New York: Citadel Press, 1965.

Klimo, Vernon, and Will Oursler. *Hemingway and Jake: An Extraordinary Friendship*. New York: Popular Library, 1972. See pp. 35–38.

Kovács, József. "Ernest Hemingway, Mati Zalka and Spain: To the Symbolic Meaning of *The Old Man and the Sea*." Acta Litteraria Academiae Scientiarum Hungaricae (Budapest) 13 (1971): 315–24.

Lagios, Socrates A. "*The Old Man and the Sea*–1932 and 1952," *Exercise Exchange* 10 (March 1963): 12–13.

Lehan, Richard. *A Dangerous Crossing: French Literary Existentialism and the Modern American Novel*. Carbondale and Edwardsville: Southern Illinois University Press, 1973.

Lewis, Robert W., Jr. *Hemingway on Love*. Austin: University of Texas Press, 1965, pp. 195–213.

Longmire, Samuel E. "Hemingway's Praise of Dick Sisler in *The Old Man and the Sea*." *American Literature* 42 (1970): 96–98.

Mansell, Darrel. "*The Old Man and the Sea* and the Computer," *Computers and the Humanities* 8 (1974), 195–206.

McLendon, James. *Papa Hemingway in Key West, 1928–1940*. New York: Popular Library, 1972. See pp. 44, 63, 125, 190.

Meador, John M., Jr. "Addendum to Hanneman: Hemingway's *The Old Man and the Sea*." *Papers of the Bibliographical Society of America* 67 (1973): 454–57.

Moloney, Michael F. "Ernest Hemingway: The Missing Third Dimension." In *Fifty Years of the American Novel*. Edited by Harold C. Gardiner. New York and London: Charles Scribner's Sons, 1952, pp. 183–96. Reprinted in Baker, ed., *Hemingway and His Critics*, pp. 180–91.

Monteiro, George. "Santiago, DiMaggio, and Hemingway: The Ageing Professionals of *The Old Man and the Sea*." *Fitzgerald/Hemingway Annual* (1975), 273–80.

Moseley, Edwin M. "Christ as the Old Champion: Hemingway's *The Old Man and the Sea*." In *Pseudonyms of Christ in the Modern Novel*. Pittsburgh: University of Pittsburgh Press, 1962, pp. 205–313.

Motola, Gabriel, "Hemingway's Code: Literature and Life." *Modern Fiction Studies* 10 (Winter 1964–65): 319–29.

Nelson, Jon E. "Religious Experience in the Fiction of Ernest Hemingway." *Dissertation Abstracts International* 31 (1970): 396A (North Carolina, Chapel Hill).

Oldsey, Bernard S. "Hemingway's Old Men." *Modern Fiction Studies* 1 (August 1955): 31–35.

Plimpton, George. "Ernest Hemingway: The Art of Fiction XXI," *The Paris Review*, no. 18 (Spring 1958), pp. 61–89.

Portuondo, José Antonio. "The Old Man and Society." *Americas* 4 (1952): 6–7, 42–44.

Prizel, Yuri. "The Critics and *The Old Man and the Sea*," *Research Studies* (Washington State University) 41 (1973), 208–16.

Rahv, Philip. "Hemingway in the 1950's." In *Image and Idea: Twenty Essays on Literary Themes*, rev. and enlarged ed., New York: New Directions, 1957, pp. 188–95.

Rosenfield, Claire. "New World, Old Myths." In *Twentieth Century Interpretations of "The Old Man and the Sea."* Edited by Katharine Jobes, pp. 41–56.

Rovit, Earl. "The Structures of the Fiction." In *Ernest Hemingway*. United States Authors Series. New York: Twayne Publishers, Inc., 1963, pp. 83–94.

Rubinstein, Annette T. "Brave and Baffled Hunter." *Mainstream* 13 (January 1960): 1–23.

Sanderson, Stewart. *Hemingway*. Writers and Critics Series. Edinburgh: Oliver and Boyd, 1961, pp. 113–18. Also published as Evergreen Pilot Book, New York, 1961.

Schorer, Mark. "With Grace under Pressure." *New Republic* 127 (October 6, 1962): 19–20. Reprinted in Baker, ed., *Critiques of Four Major Novels*, pp. 132–34.

Schwartz, Delmore. "The Fiction of Ernest Hemingway: Moral Historian of the American Dream." *Perspectives USA*, no. 13 (Autumn 1955), pp. 70–88. Pages 82–88 reprinted as *"The Old Man and the Sea* and the American Dream" in Jobes, ed., *Twentieth Century Interpretations of "The Old Man and the Sea,"* pp. 97–102.

Scoville, Samuel. "The *Weltanschauung* of Steinbeck and Hemingway: An Analysis of Themes." *English Journal* 56 (January 1967): 60–63, 66.

Singh, Satyanarain. "The Psychology of Heroic Living in *The Old Man and the Sea," Osmania Journal of English Studies* 10 (1973), 7–16.

Sojka, Gregory S. "Hemingway as Angler-Artist." *Lost Generation Journal* 3 (1975),.12–13.

Spector, Robert D. "Hemingway's *The Old Man and the Sea." The Explicator* 11 (March 1953), item 38, no page listed.

Stephens, Robert O. "Hemingway's Old Man and the Iceberg." *Modern Fiction Studies* 7 (Winter 1961-62): 295–304.

Sylvester, Bickford. "Hemingway's Extended Vision: *The Old Man and the Sea." PMLA* 81 (March 1966): 130–38. Reprinted in Jobes, ed., *Twentieth Century Interpretations of "The Old Man and the Sea,"* pp. 81–96.

–––. " 'They Went Through This Fiction Every Day': Informed Illusion in *The Old Man and the Sea." Modern Fiction Studies* 12 (Winter 1966–67): 473–79.

Toynbee, Philip. "Hemingway." *Encounter* 17 (October 1961): 86–88.

Ueno, Naozo. "An Oriental View of *The Old Man and the Sea." The East-West Review* (Doshisha University, Kyoto, Japan) 2 (Spring–Summer 1965): 67–76.

Wagner, Linda W. "The Poem of Santiago and Manolin." *Modern Fiction Studies* 19 (1973-74): 517–29.

Waldmeir, Joseph. "Confiteor Hominem: Ernest Hemingway's Religion of Man," *Papers of the Michigan Academy of Sciences, Arts, and Letters* (Ann Arbor: University of Michigan Press) 42 (1957): 349–56. Reprinted in Baker, ed., *Ernest Hemingway: Critiques of Four Major Novels*, pp. 144–49; and in Weeks, ed., *Hemingway: A Collection of Critical Essays*, pp. 161–68.

Warner, Stephan D. "Hemingway's *The Old Man and the Sea." Explicator* 33 (1974), item 9.

Weeks, Robert P. "Fakery in *The Old Man and the Sea." College English* 24 (December 1962): 188–92. Reprinted in Jobes, ed., *Twentieth Century Interpretations of "The Old Man and the Sea,"* pp. 34–41.

–––, ed. *Hemingway: A Collection of Critical Essays*. Twentieth Century Views. Englewood Cliffs, New Jersey: Prentice-Hall, Inc., 1962.

Wells, Arvin R. "A Ritual of Transfiguration: *The Old Man and the Sea*." *The University Review* 30 (December 1963): 95-101. Reprinted in Jobes, ed., *Twentieth Century Interpretations of "The Old Man and the Sea,"* pp. 56-64.
White, William. "Addendum to Hanneman: Hemingway's *The Old Man and the Sea*." *Papers of the Bibliographical Society of America* 62 (1968): 613-14.
Wylder, Delbert E. "*The Old Man and the Sea:* The Hero as Saint and Sinner." In *Hemingway's Heroes.* Albuquerque: The University of New Mexico Press, 1969, pp. 199-222.
Yoshida, Hiroshige. "Comments on *The Bear* and *The Old Man and the Sea*." *Hiroshima Studies in English Language and Literature* 18 (1971), 69-77.
Young, Philip. "Death and Transfiguration," and "Afterword." In *Ernest Hemingway: A Reconsideration.* University Park: The Pennsylvania State University Press, 1966, pp. 123-33, 274-75. Reprinted as "*The Old Man and the Sea:* Vision/Revision" in Jobes, ed., *Twentieth Century Interpretations of "The Old Man and the Sea,"* pp. 18-27.
Zabel, Morton D. *Craft and Character in Modern Fiction.* New York: Viking, 1957, pp. 321-26.

INDEX